Piano Scales, Chords, and Arpeggios Book

by Peter Vogl

Copyright 2024 by Watch & Learn, Inc. 1st Edition
ALL RIGHTS RESERVED. Any copying, arranging, or adapting of this work without the
consent of the owner is an infringement of copyright.

About This Book

Inspiration for this book began several years ago when I decided to work on my piano skills. The scale and arpeggio books available didn't cover everything I needed and in many cases seemed more difficult than they had to be. In this book, we've included many items I felt would help piano players progress easier and further.

In each major and minor section, there are five note scales as well as one and two octave scales. The five note scale is a great beginning path for the piano player and also a good exercise. The arpeggios have a one octave arpeggio as well as two octave arpeggios with inversions. The one octave arpeggio is a great starting point for the new piano player. The scales also have crossovers and crossunders notated by brackets showing when the shift occurs. This can be hugely helpful for anyone just learning that scale.

I've also included the harmonic and melodic minor scales, not just the natural minor. The scales, cadences, and arpeggios have each note fingered to make them easier to read. This book also has a pentatonic scale section which couldn't be found in other scale and arpeggio books. Hopefully you will find this book helpful as you practice piano. Each element in this book is important for the well rounded piano player.

About The Author

Peter Vogl has been a performer, producer and instructor in the music business for over thirty years . He studied classical guitar in college at the University of Georgia under the tutelage of John Sutherland and at James Madison University.

Peter played the club circuit in Atlanta as a soloist and with a multitude of bands. Peter has performed on stage with talents such as Michael Bolton, Cee-Lo, Kelly Price, Steve Vai, Earl Klugh, Sharon Isbon, and Sleepy Brown. In the 90's Peter met Jan Smith and began to play with the Jan Smith Band performing on several of her CDs. In 2001 Peter moved into Jan Smith Studios where he continues to teach and do session work with local and national talent.

Peter has also written many music instructional books for Watch & Learn Inc. that can be found on Amazon.com.

For any technical or sales questions about this book, please email sales@cvls.com.

Table of Contents

Getting Started 4
  The Keyboard 5
  Notation 6
  Key Signatures 8
  Scales 9
  Relative Major and Minor 10
  Key Signatures 11
  Enharmonics 12
  Chord Qualities and Symbols 13
  Arpeggios and Chords 14
  The Cadence 15
  Fingerings and Shifts 16
  Tips For Using this Book 17
Major Keys 19
  C Major 20
  G Major 23
  D Major 27
  A Major 31
  E Major 35
  B Major 39
  F Major 43
  B♭ Major 47
  E♭ Major 51
  A♭ Major 55
  D♭ Major 59
  G♭ Major 63
Major Cadences with Dominant 7th 67
Minor Keys 71
  A Minor 72
  E Minor 75
  B Minor 79
  F♯ Minor 83
  C♯ Minor 87
  G♯ Minor 91
  D Minor 95
  G Minor 99
  C Minor 103
  C Minor 103
  F Minor 107
  B♭ Minor 111
  E♭ Minor 115

Harmonic Minor 119
  A Harmonic Minor 120
  E Harmonic Minor 121
  B Harmonic Minor 122
  F♯ Harmonic Minor 123
  C♯ Harmonic Minor 124
  G♯ Harmonic Minor 125
  D Harmonic Minor 126
  G Harmonic Minor 127
  C Harmonic Minor 128
  F Harmonic Minor 129
  B♭ Harmonic Minor 130
  E♭ Harmonic Minor 131
Minor Cadences with Dominant 7th 132
Melodic Minor Scales 136
Chromatic Scales 140
Pentatonic Scales 142
Minor Pentatonic Scales 146
Enharmonic Keys 150

Getting Started

The Keyboard 5
Notation 6
Key Signatures 8
Scales 9
Relative Major and Minor 10
Key Signatures 11
Enharmonics 12
Chord Qualities and Symbols 13
Arpeggios and Chords 14
The Cadence 15
Fingerings and Shifts 16
Tips For Using this Book 17

The Keyboard

The white keys are natural notes and the black keys are accidentals, or sharps and flats.

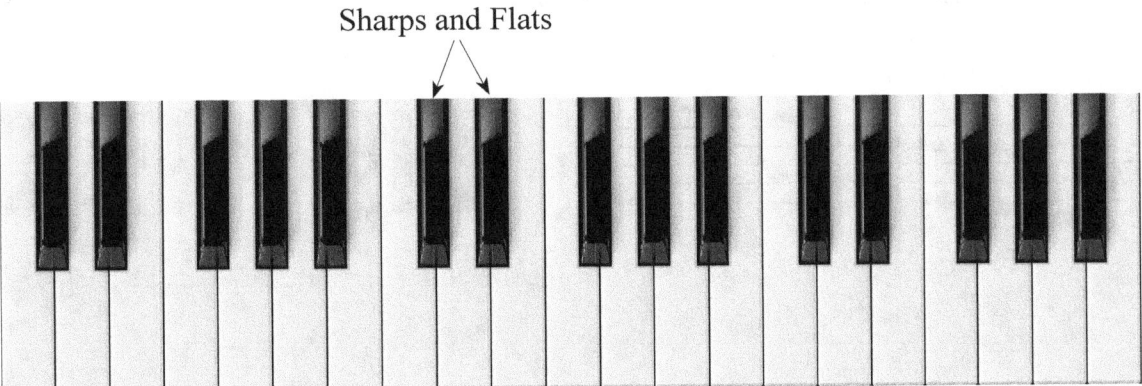

Fingers

The finger numbers for piano are identical for both hands. The thumb is always number 1 and the pinky is number 5.

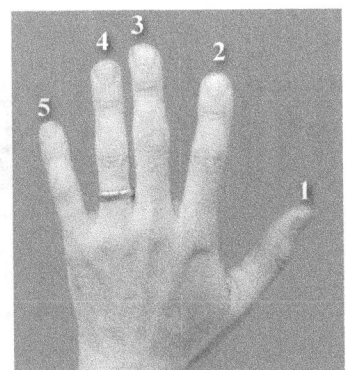

Left Hand

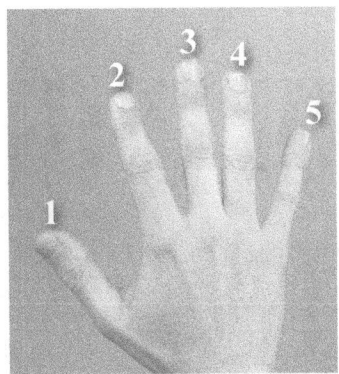

Right Hand

Notation

Piano notations uses two clefs: the Treble and the Bass Clef. Starting on middle C, here are the natural notes on the treble clef.

Starting one octave below middle C, here are the notes on the bass clef.

 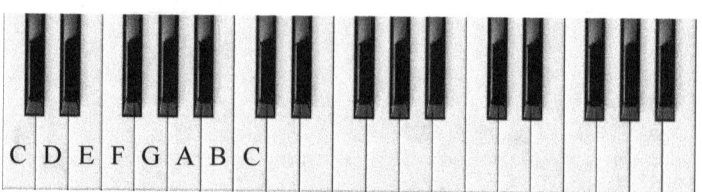

The black keys on the piano are the sharps and flats. A sharp note is one key on the keyboard higher (half step) and a flat is one key on the keyboard lower (half step).

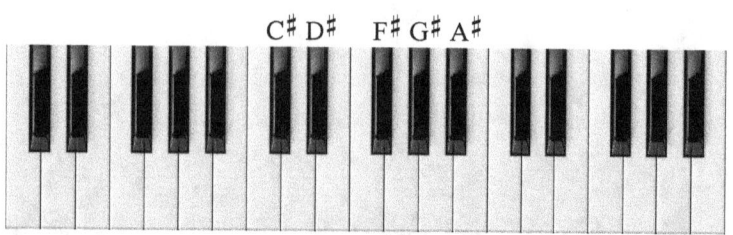 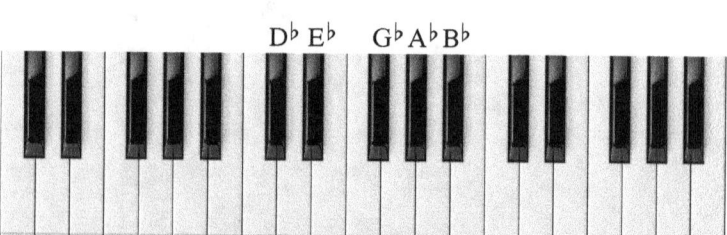

Rhythm Notation

A whole note lasts four beats. A half note lasts for two beats. The quarter note lasts one beat and the eighth note lasts half a beat or is twice as fast as a quarter note. The sixteenth note is twice as fast as the eighth note.

The speed or tempo at which you play these scales should be decided by you. The rhythmic notation is not intended to imply any speed. Practice at whatever tempo is working for you.

Music notation is usually divided up into measures or bars and the time signature tells us how many beats are in a bar. There are a variety of time signatures, but throughout this book, we will be using 4/4 time. This means each bar gets 4 quarter notes or 4 beats to a measure and each beat may be subdivided to faster notes.

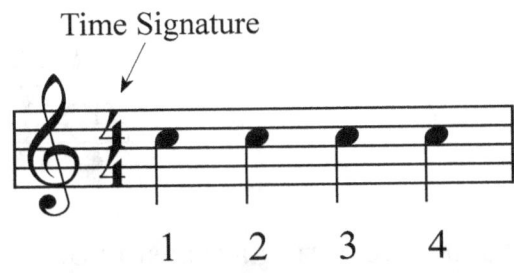

When chords or several notes played at a time are indicated, the notes are stacked on top of each other.

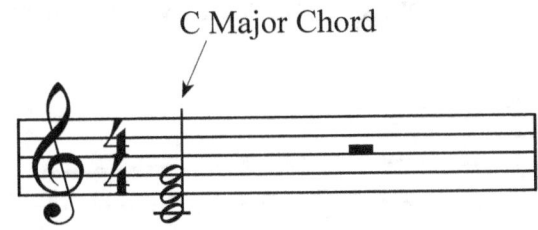

Key Signatures

A key signature tells us what sharps and flats to play throughout the exercise or song. Each major and minor key will have a different key signature. The examples below, from left to right, show C Major with no sharps or flats, G major with one sharp, B♭ major with two flats in the key signature.

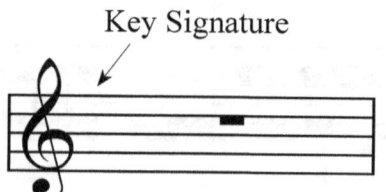
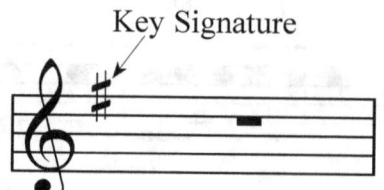

Accidentals

It is often necessary to add or take away sharps and flats from the key signature. In this case, we include accidentals. A sharp will tell us to play a note one half step higher. A half step means one key to the right or left on the piano whether it is a black or white key.

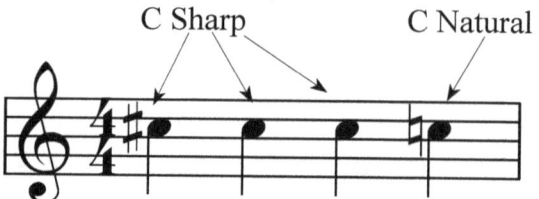

A flat will tell us to play a note a half step lower or one key to the left on the piano.

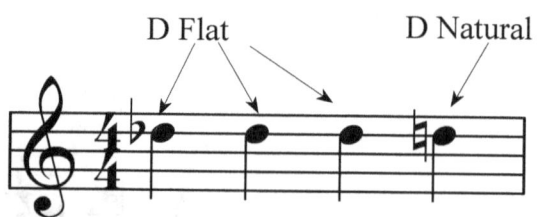

An accidental is only needed once during a measure or bar and that note is to be played in that position for the rest of the bar. In the next bar, that note reverts back to the original key signature. In the example above, the D is flat and is then played flat for the rest of the bar unless otherwise indicated by a natural sign. In a few cases it is necessary to use a double sharp. In the example below, the F is double sharped, which means you are playing the note G followed by the note G sharp (G is sharped in key signature).

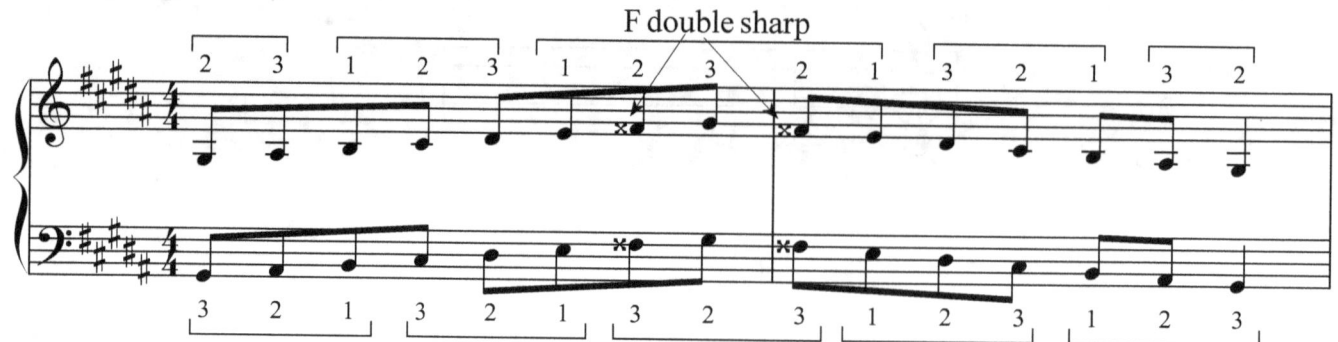

8

Scales

A scale is a series of single notes. A scale may have a few or up to twelve different notes. For example, the pentatonic scale has five notes while the diatonic scale has seven. The chromatic scale includes twelve different notes.

Major and Minor Scales

The Major scale is perhaps the most important scale to know, especially for music theory purposes. The minor scale is a similar scale with a darker sound. Both are seven note scales and every key we play in is based on a major or minor scale. From the low C (first note of scale) to the higher C (last note in scale) in the example below is called an octave and it is in the key of C.

C D E F G A B C

The Chromatic Scale

The Chromatic scale moves by half steps. It includes all of the notes on the piano. Simply play the next key on the keyboard going up or down, one after the other including the black and white keys. The example below is a one octave chromatic scale.

The Pentatonic Scale

The Pentatonic scale is a five note scale that is used heavily in improvisation and has its own unique sound or flavor. Think of it as a shortened major or minor scale. Below is an example of a C major pentatonic scale

Relative Major and Minor

For every major scale or major key, there is a minor key with exactly the same notes. They start and end on different notes, but include the same seven pitches. These scales are called *relative* major and minor scales. Below is an example using C major and A minor. They are considered relative major and minor.

C Major Scale   A Minor Scale

The Three Minor Scales

There are three variations of the minor scale: Natural minor, Harmonic minor, and Melodic minor. Think of Harmonic minor and Melodic minor as variations of the Natural minor scale. The Harmonic minor has a raised or sharp 7th degree (note) of the minor scale. The Melodic minor scale has a raised 6th and 7th degree ascending, but plays the Natural minor scale descending. Since the chords in any key are built from the notes in the scale, Harmonic and Melodic minor have a different set of chords than the natural minor scale. Each of these scales is covered in this book.

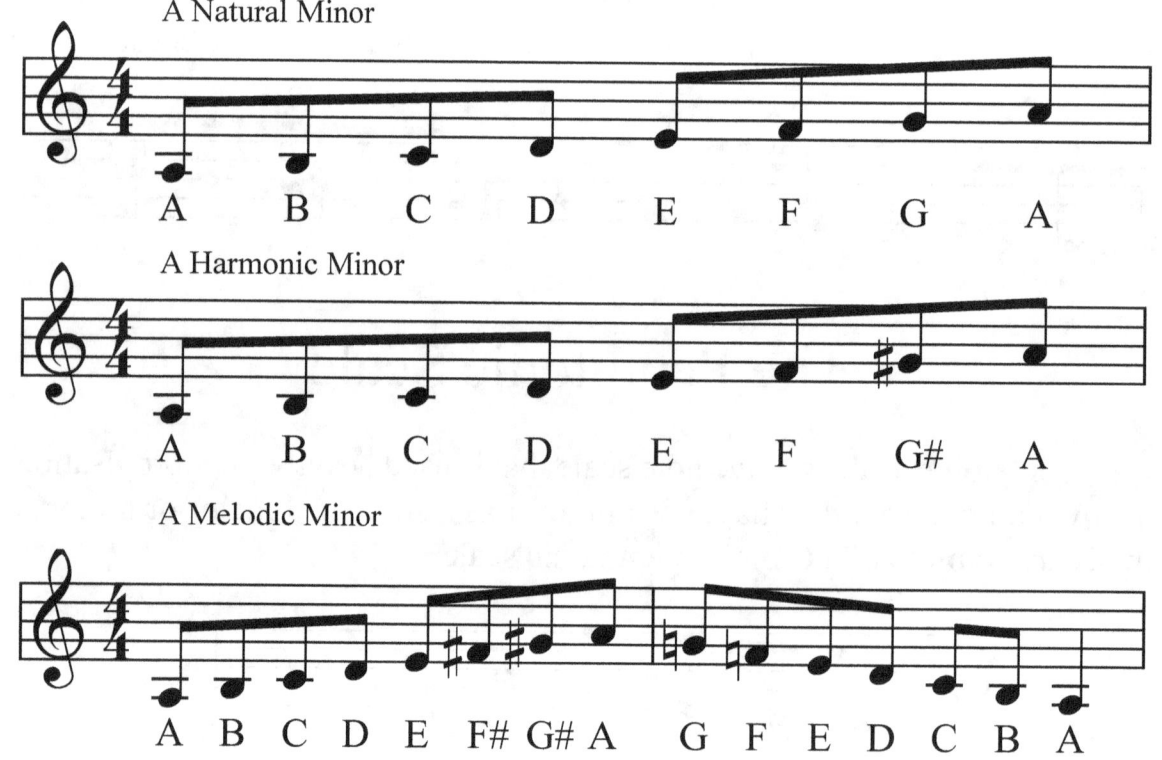

Key Signatures

Below is a list of the key signatures. Remember that for every major key there is a relative key with the same key signature. It would be helpful to memorize these.

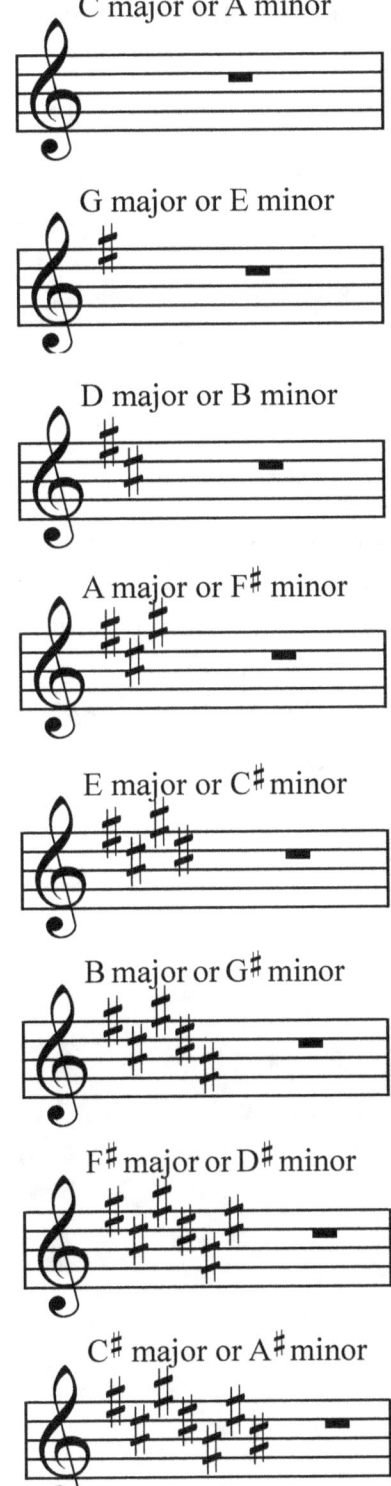
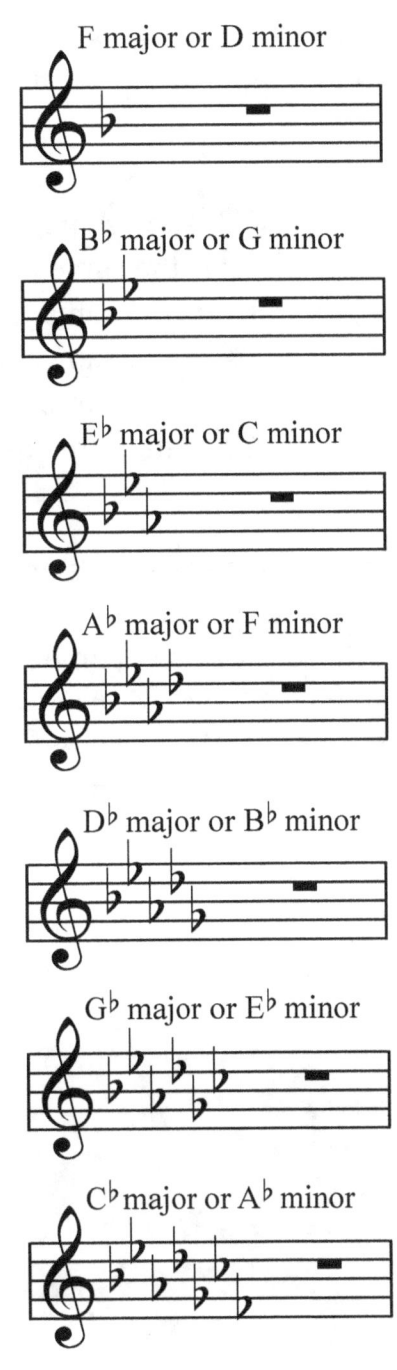

Enharmonics

Pitches, chords, or scales that are identical but can be written using either sharps or flats are enharmonic. For example, C♭ and B are identical notes but can be written either way. Since they are identical, you will find them written only one way in this book. They are the same scales and chords so the fingering is entirely the same regardless of how they are notated.

> C♭ is the same as B
> E♯ is the same as F
> D♯ is the same as E♭
> A♯ is the same as B♭
> G♯ is the same as A♭
> C♯ is the same as D♭

Where this book uses sharps or flats to notate a chord, key, or scale is determined by the relative major and minor relationship. As you play through the major and minor keys, these choices become more understandable. The enharmonic equivalent is noted in many of the sections of this book as an aid. Remember the scales/chords and fingering are identical written either way so you are practicing the same scales/chords regardless of whether they are written using sharps or flats.

Chord Qualities and Symbols

There are four chord qualities or "food groups" of chords. Major, minor, augmented, and diminished.

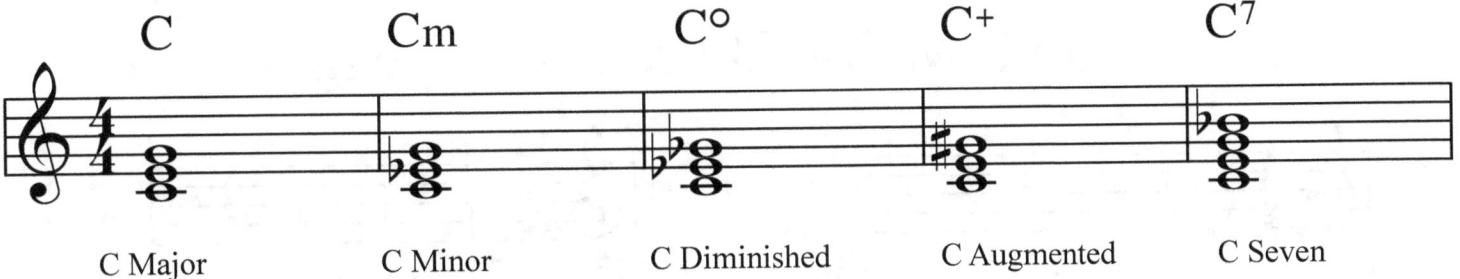

The major chord needs no symbol. The minor chord will have a small "m" next to the chord name. The diminished chord has a small circle and also may be written with the abbreviation "dim". The augmented chord has a plus symbol and may also be written with the abbreviation "aug". The seven chord, when major, will have a "7" next to the chord name.

If a chord is sharped or flatted, the sharp or flat will appear before the symbol or descriptor. For example, C#m or C♭+. C sharp minor is a half step higher than Cm and C♭+ is a half step lower than C+.

Arpeggios and Chords

Generally, a chord is three or more different notes played at the same time. A three note chord may also be called a triad. An arpeggio is a chord broken up and played one note at a time.

The C Major Chord and Arpeggio

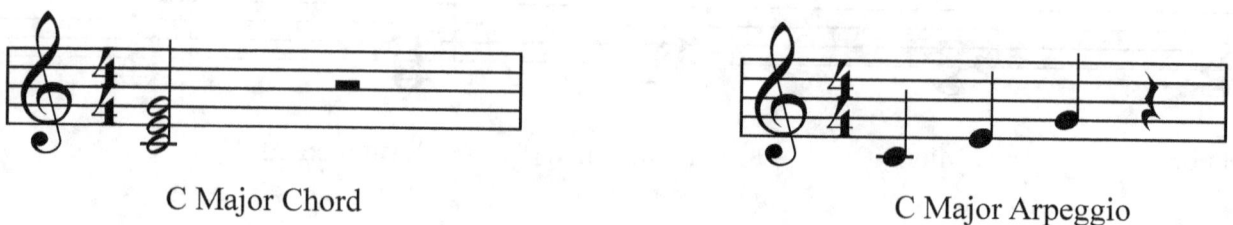

C Major Chord   C Major Arpeggio

Root Position, First Inversion, Second Inversion

A chord may be played in several positions. When the note that names the chord is the lowest note, it is in root position. In the example below, C is the root of the chord, E is the third, and G is the fifth. When the third of the chord is lowest it is in first inversion. When the fifth of the chord is the lowest note it is in second inversion.

C Major Chord Root Position   C Major Chord First Inversion   C Major Chord Second Inversion

Chord Progressions

A chord progression is a series of chords. Chords within a chord progression are commonly given numbers representing where they fall within the key.

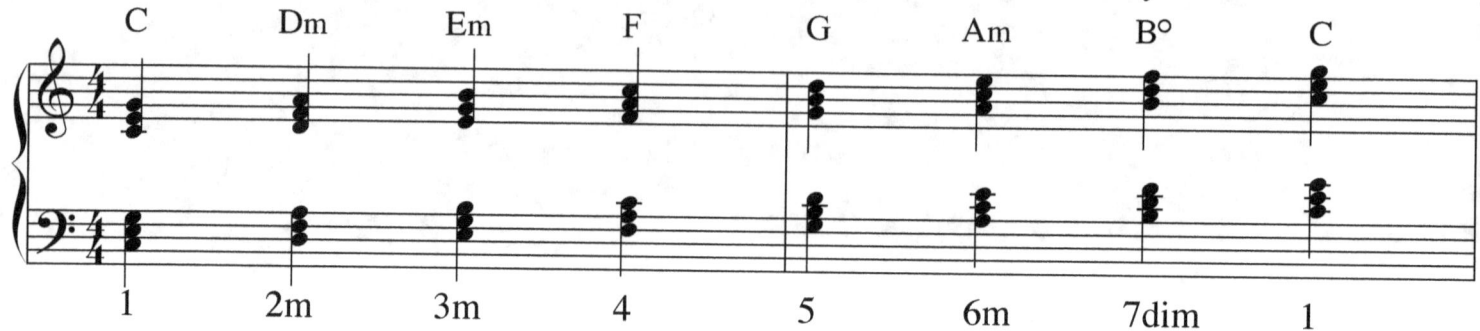

14

The Cadence

A cadence is a common chord progression that gives a sense of completion to the progression. In this example below, the chord progression is a 1, 4, 1, 5, 1. The G chord (5) to C chord(1) is considered a strong or perfect cadence. The numbers in this example refer to the fingerings to use. Remember however, fingerings are suggestions and not rules. Try them and then over time see what works for you.

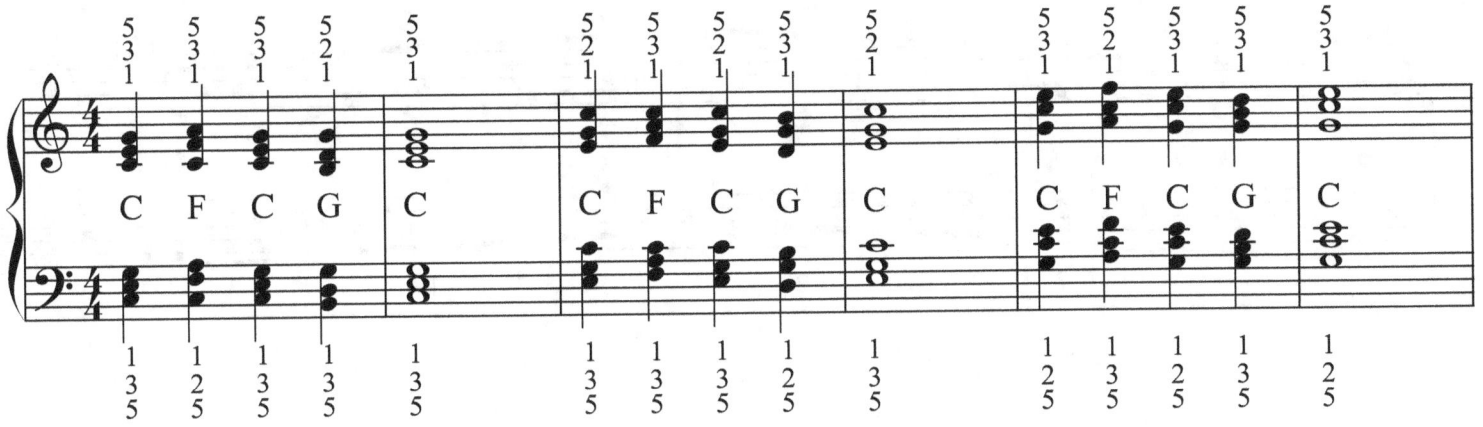

The Dominant 7th Chord

A dominant 7th chord is a chord consisting of four notes. It has a root, third, fifth, and a flat seven. This chord naturally occurs when adding the seventh to the fifth chord in a major key, harmonic or melodic minor scale. The seventh adds "tension" to the chord, which is then commonly resolved by playing the one chord immediately following. In the example below, the D7 chord is a dominant 7th chord which is resolved when playing the G. This is an extremely common sound in music.

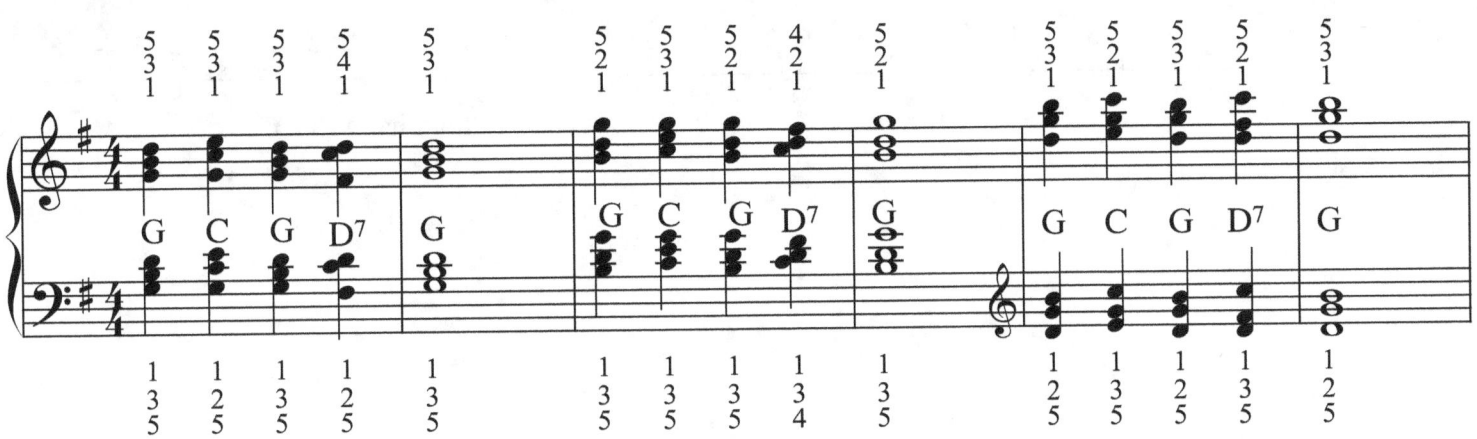

Fingerings and Shifts

The fingerings are notated by numbers above or below the staff. The right hand is playing the top staff and the left hand is playing the bottom staff. We have included brackets to indicate when to shift hand positions or when to cross with your thumb or finger.

Clef Change

Pay very close attention to the clef signs as they frequently change throughout this book. This is due to the range of scales and arpeggios. It would otherwise be very difficult to read the notation.

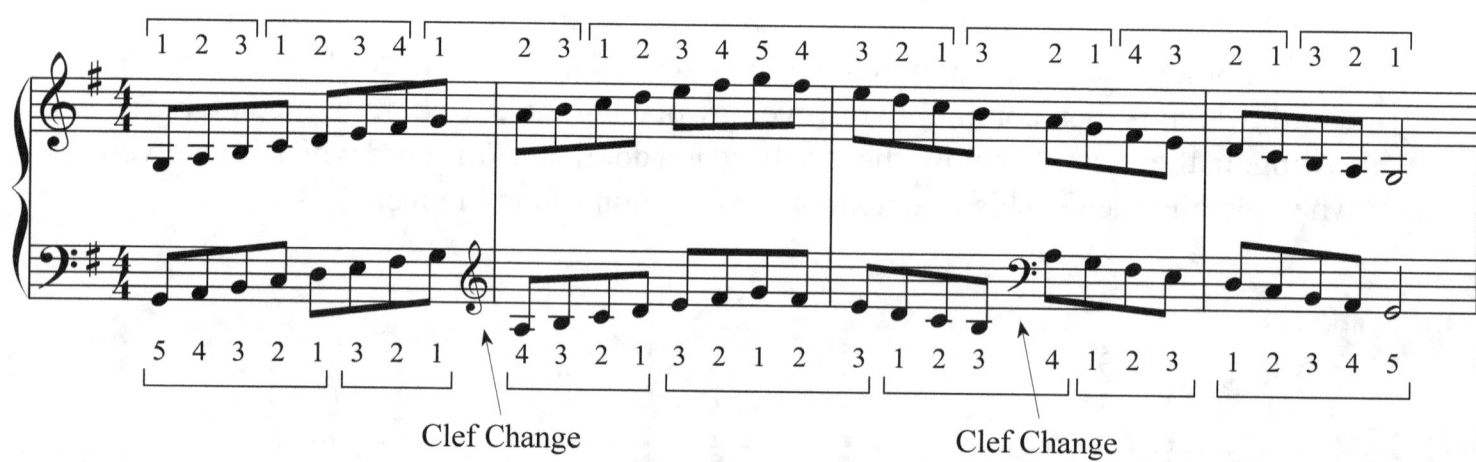

Tips For Using this Book

When practicing the scales, arpeggios, chords, or any exercises in the book, practice very slowly at first. Only after you are comfortable playing what you are working on should you attempt to speed it up. The notation does not indicate speed. Pick a speed that works for you.

In this book, you will commonly find one or two octaves of the scale or exercise in an upper and lower staff. The upper staff should be played with the right hand and the lower staff with the left hand. You do not have to play these together. Practice either hand on their own and then try both hands together.

We have included a five note scale for the major and minor keys in this book. Although this isn't considered a complete scale, it is a great exercise to play and work on. The shifts in the one octave or two octave scales may seem complex for the new player, so the five note scale is a great way to start. Practicing it at faster speeds can also improve speed and dexterity.

Five Note Scale

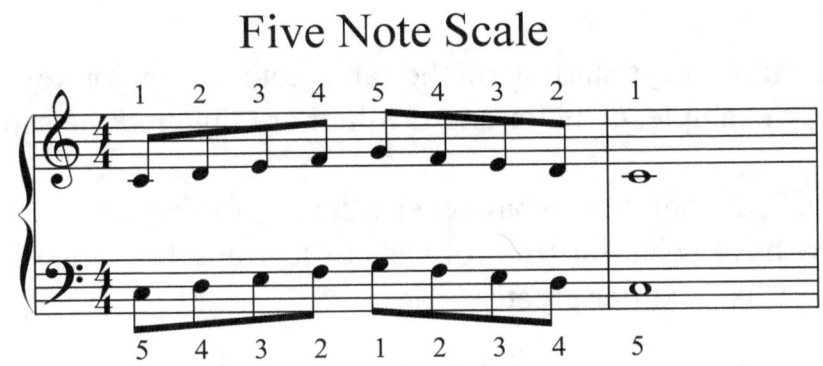

Due to the range that two octave scales and arpeggios cover, it is necessary to include clef changes. Pay very close attention to the clef changes while practicing.

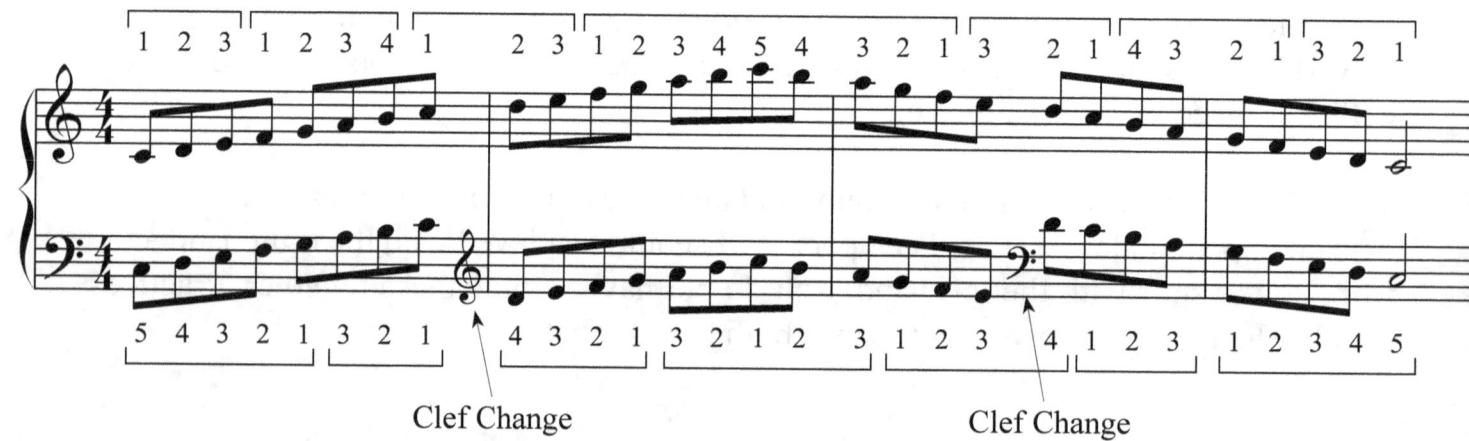

It may make it easier to learn fingerings of the scales if you see the similarities that many have. Remember that fingerings are optional.

Major scales starting on the white keys all have the same fingering and shifts except for B♭ and F. Beginner students may find it easier to start with these scales. Just remember to practice the other keys as soon as you are able.

One Octave	1-2-3-1-2-3-4-5
Two Octave	1-2-3-1-2-3-4-1-2-3-1-2-3-4-5

Most major scales starting on a black key will start with the 2nd finger of the right hand. Most major scales starting on a black key will start with the 3rd finger of the left hand.

In most cases, minor keys starting on the same note as a major key will have the same fingering. For example, C major and C minor are fingered the same.

Chromatic and Pentatonic Scales have even less rules for fingerings. The pentatonic scales in this book have been fingered for ease of learning but when implemented, fingerings will most likely differ greatly.

Once again, the fingerings for Chords and Arpeggios used here are merely suggestions offered for ease of learning. Hand size and ability to stretch with either hand may suggest variations.

Major Keys

C Major

C Major	20
G Major	23
D Major	27
A Major	31
E Major	35
B Major	39
F Major	43
B♭ Major	47
E♭ Major	51
A♭ Major	55
D♭ Major	59
G♭ Major	63

Note - The Major keys are presented in order of the number of sharps and flats in the key (C no sharps, G 1 sharp, D 2 sharps, etc.).

Key of C Major

Five Note Scale

One Octave Scale

Two Octave Scale

Contrary Motion Scale

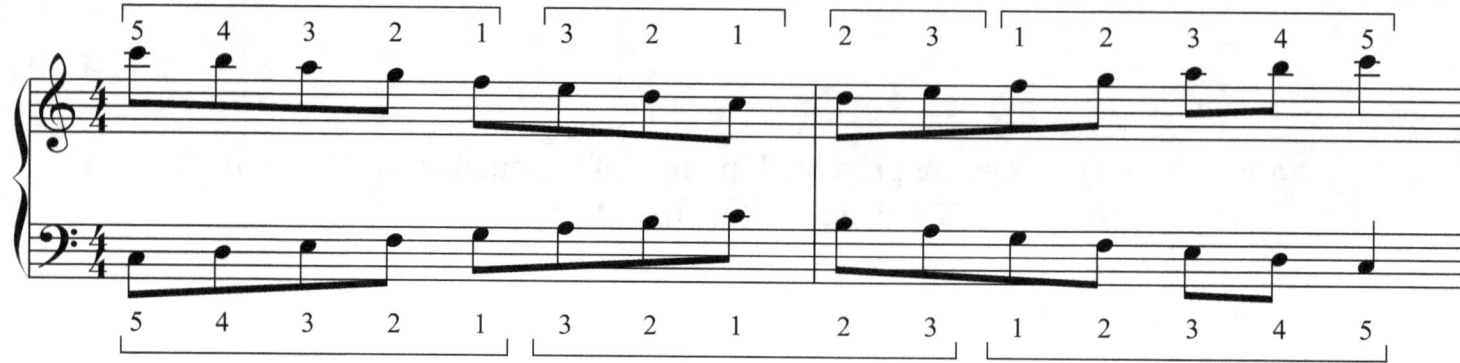

C Major Chord and Inversions

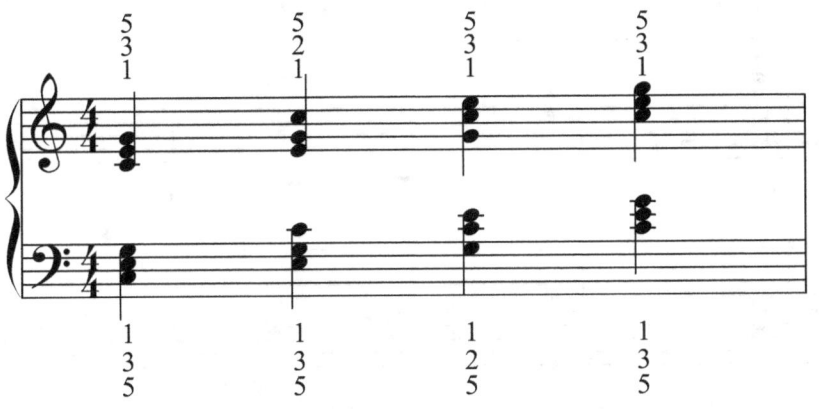

Triads in the Key of C Major

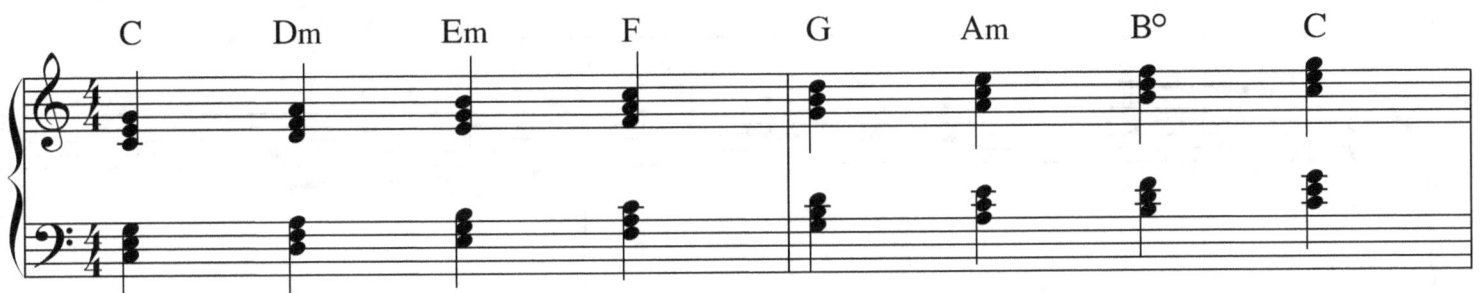

1,4,5 Chord Progression in the Key of C (Cadences)

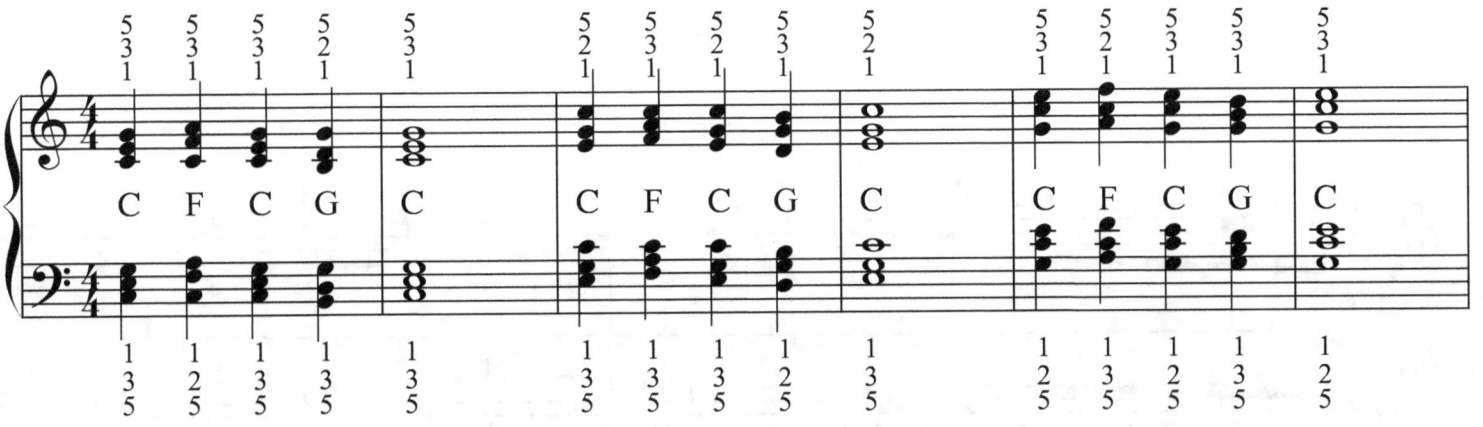

One Octave C Major Arpeggio

Two Octave C Major Arpeggios and Inversions

Remember that fingerings are suggestions and not rules. Practicing with consistent fingerings will help you memorize the scales and develop muscle memory.

G Major

Key of G Major

Five Note Scale

One Octave Scale

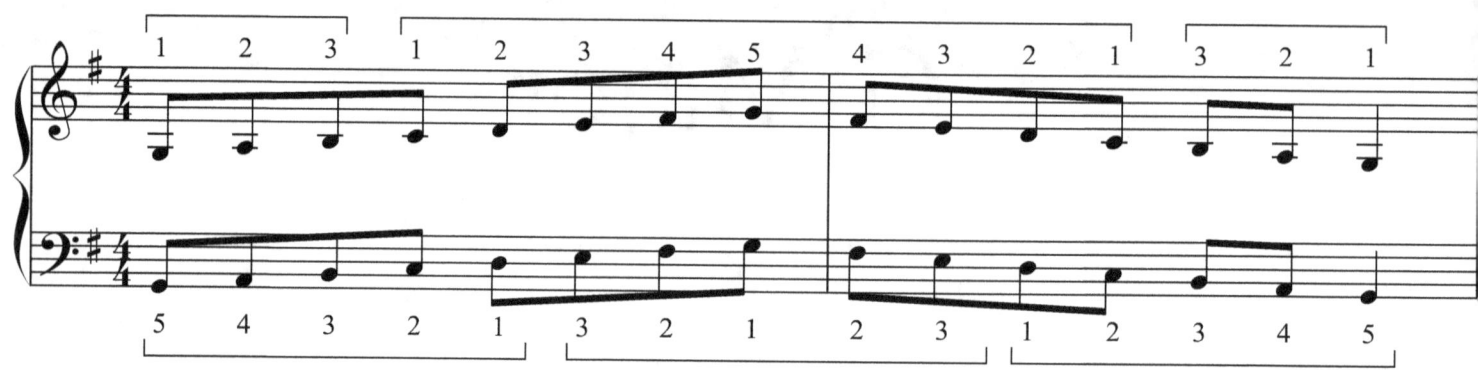

Two Octave Scale

Contrary Motion Scale

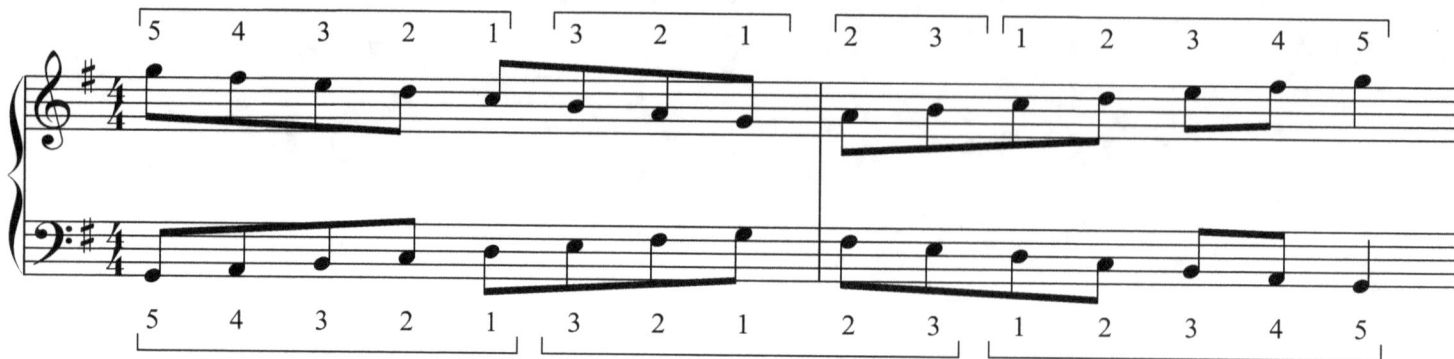

G Major Chord and Inversions

Triads in the Key of G Major

1,4,5 Chord Progression in the Key of G (Cadences)

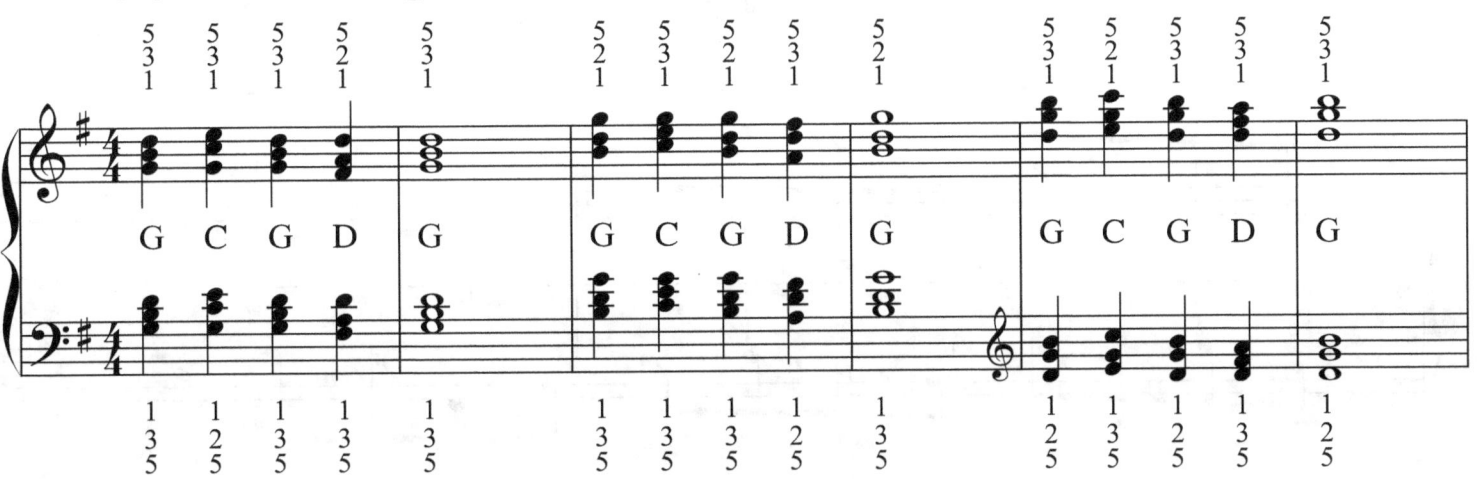

One Octave G Major Arpeggio

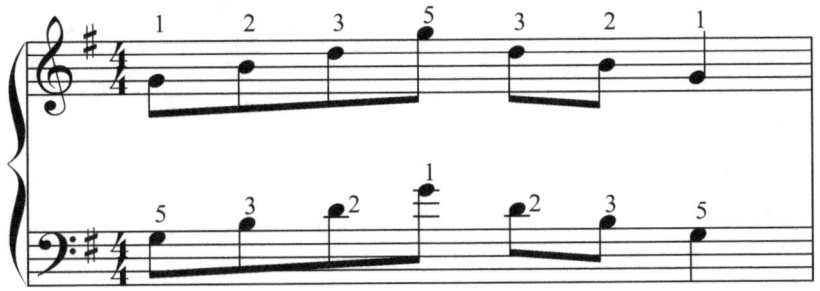

Two Octave G Major Arpeggios and Inversions

D Major

Key of D Major

Five Note Scale

One Octave Scale

Two Octave Scale

Contrary Motion Scale

D Major Chord and Inversions

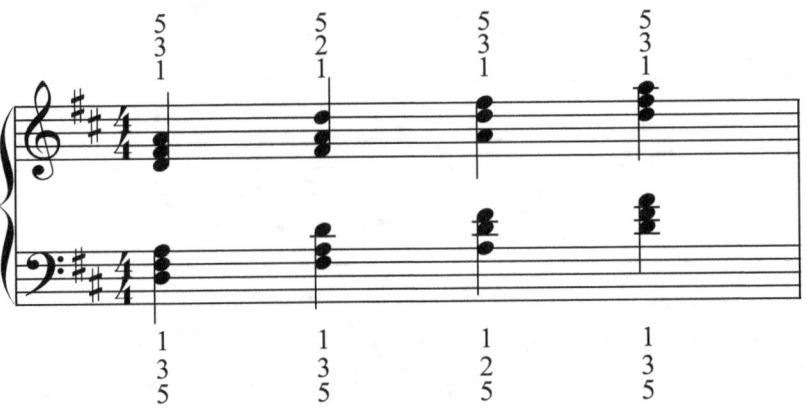

Triads in the Key of D Major

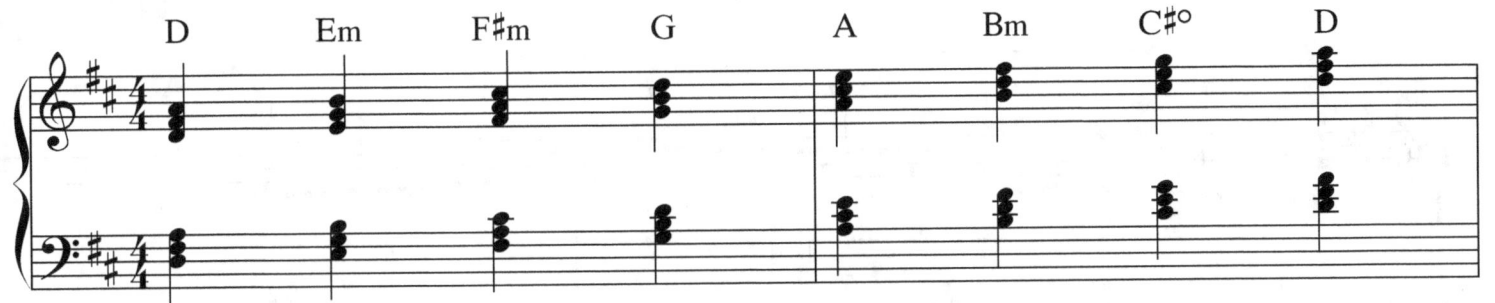

1,4,5 Chord Progression in the Key of D (Cadences)

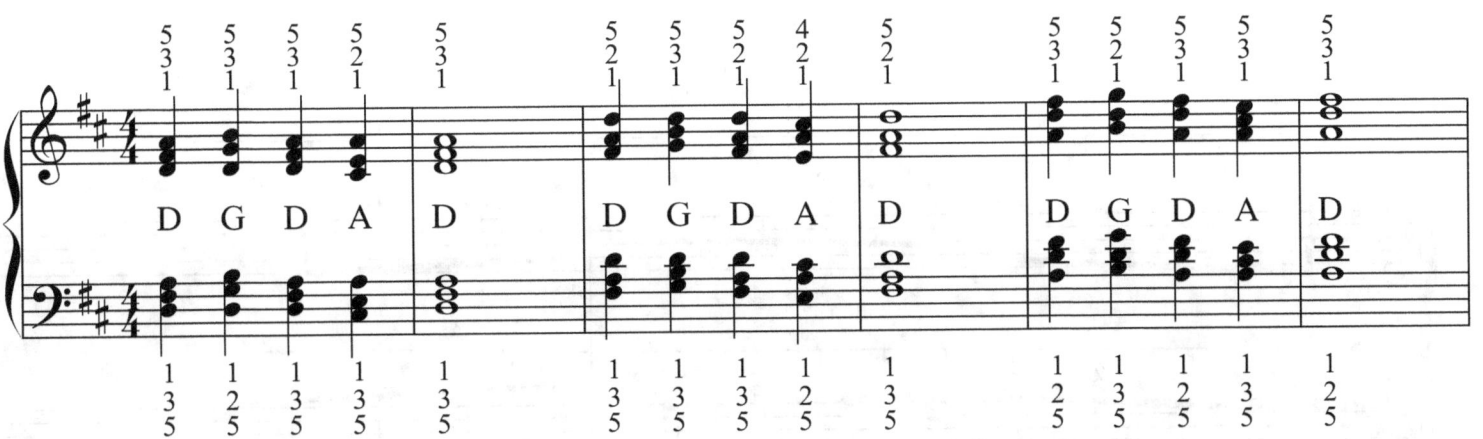

One Octave D Major Arpeggio

Two Octave D Major Arpeggios and Inversions

30

A Major

Key of A Major

Five Note Scale

One Octave Scale

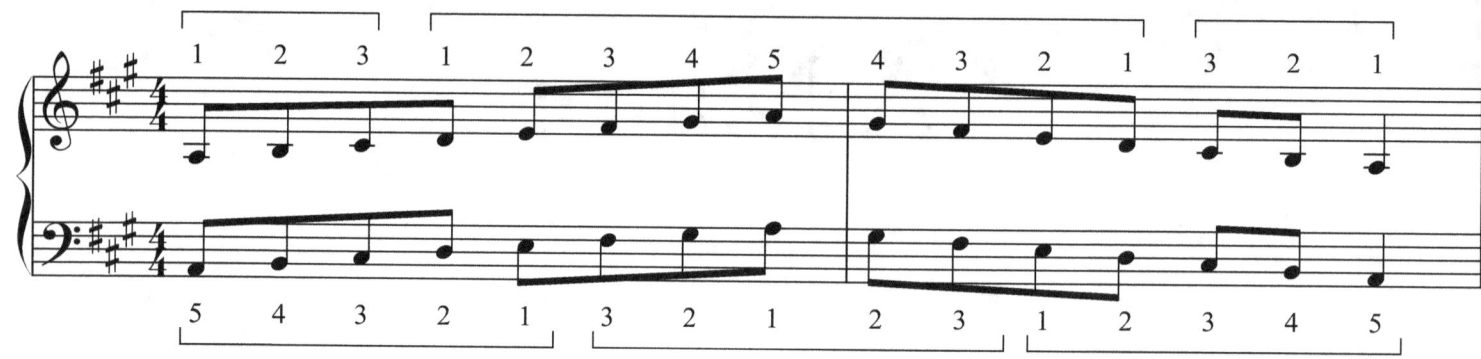

Two Octave Scale

Contrary Motion Scale

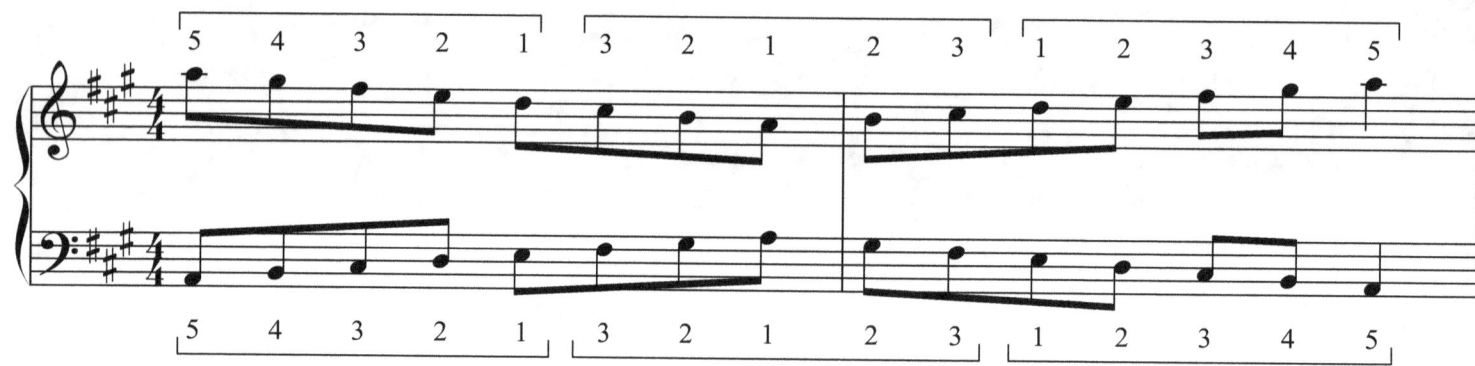

A Major Chord and Inversions

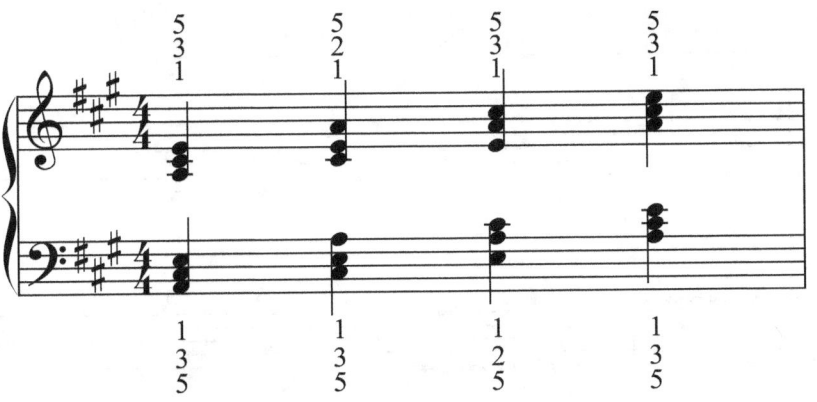

Triads in the Key of A Major

1,4,5 Chord Progression in the Key of A (Cadences)

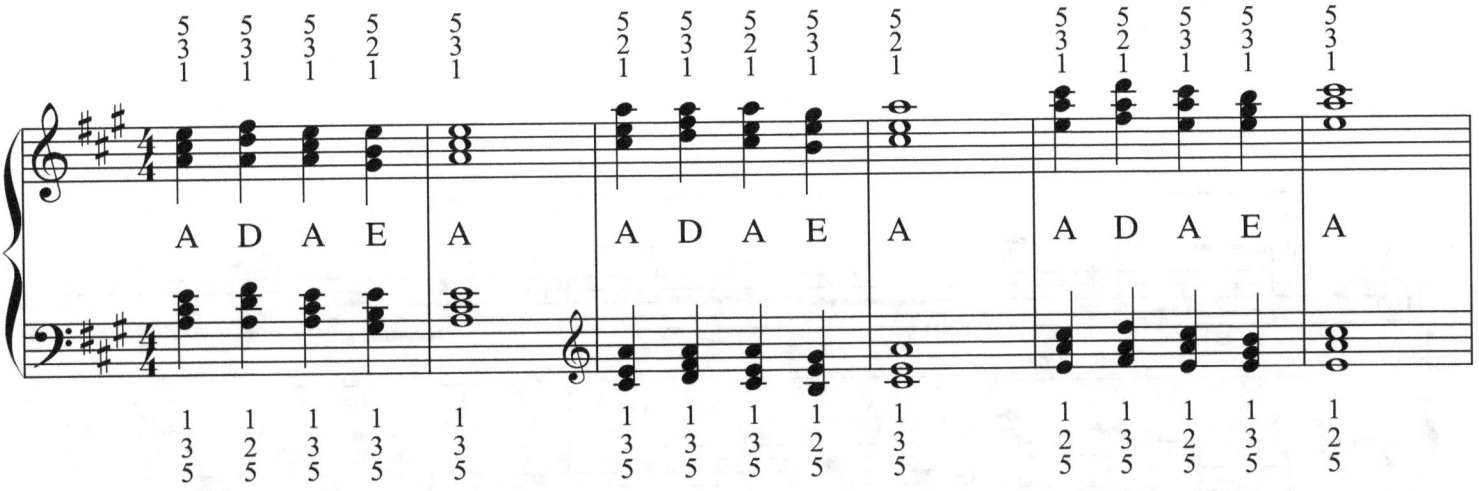

One Octave A Major Arpeggio

Two Octave A Major Arpeggios and Inversions

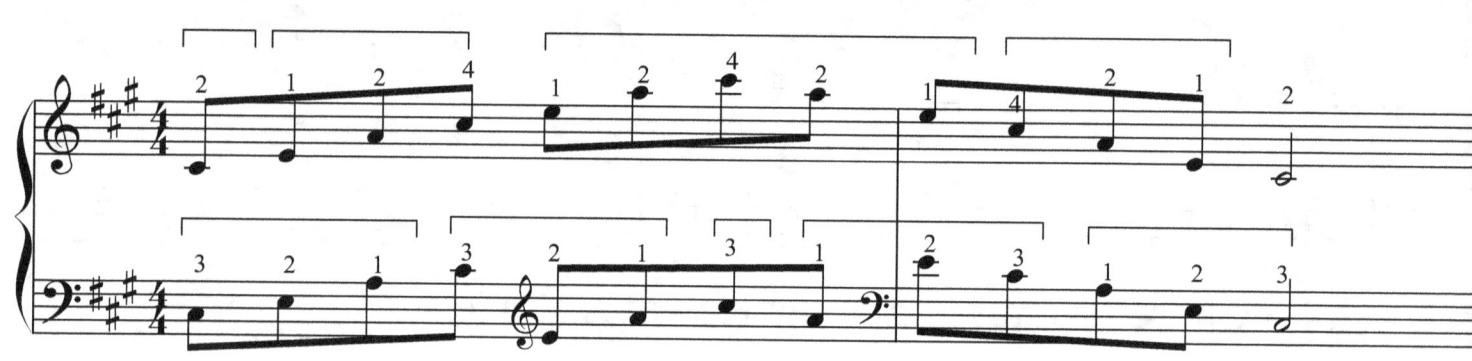

E Major

Key of E Major

Five Note Scale

One Octave Scale

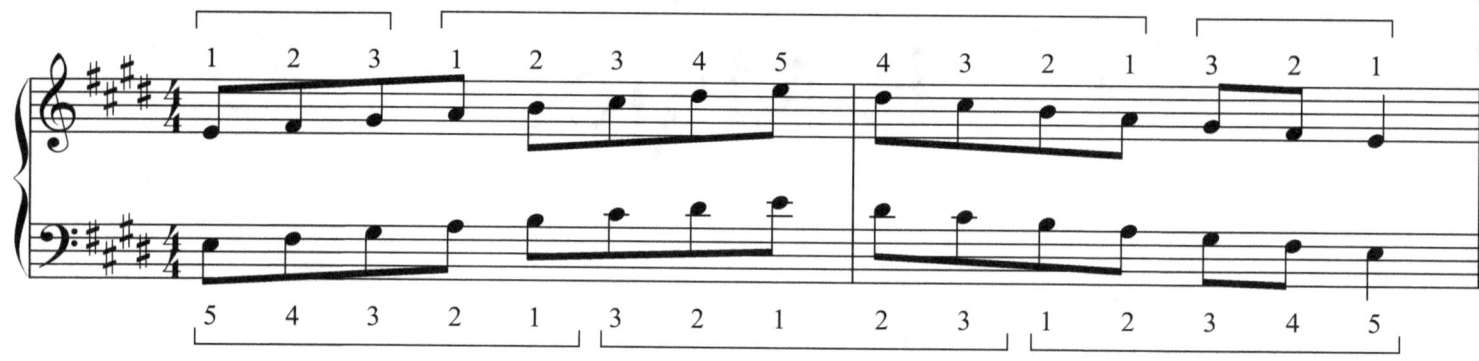

Two Octave Scale

Contrary Motion Scale

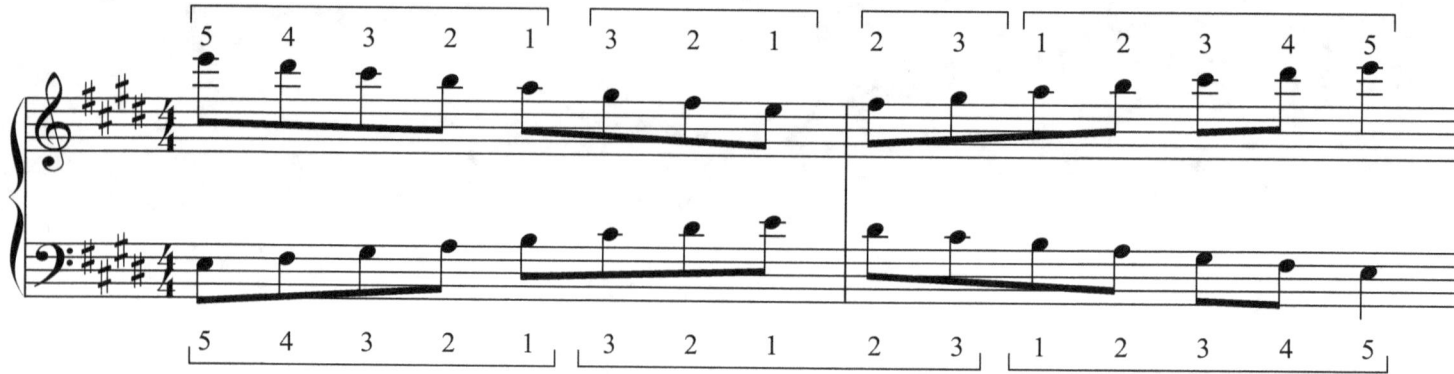

E Major Chord and Inversions

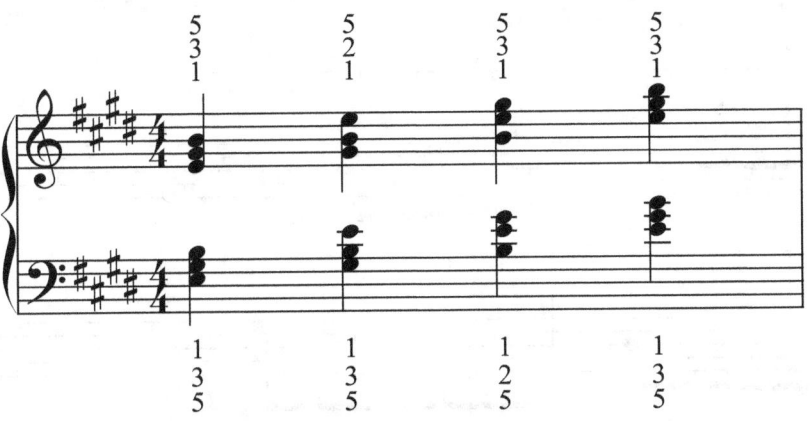

Triads in the Key of E Major

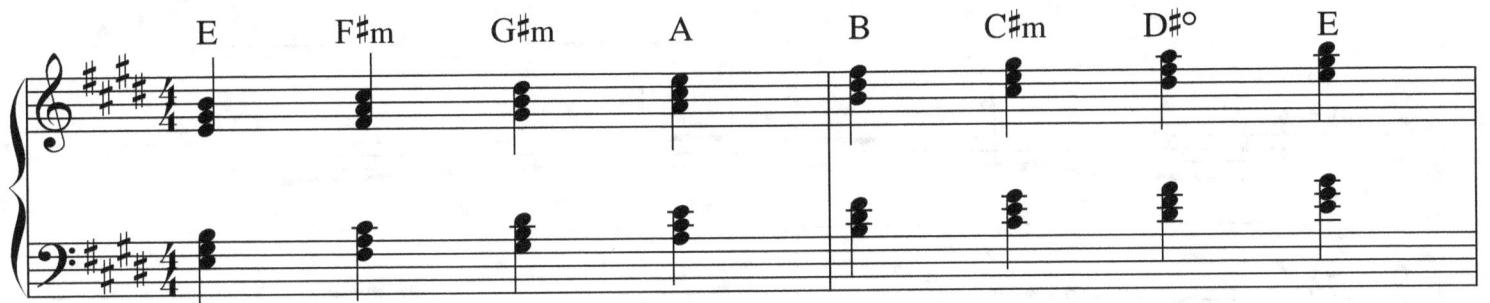

1,4,5 Chord Progression in the Key of E (Cadences)

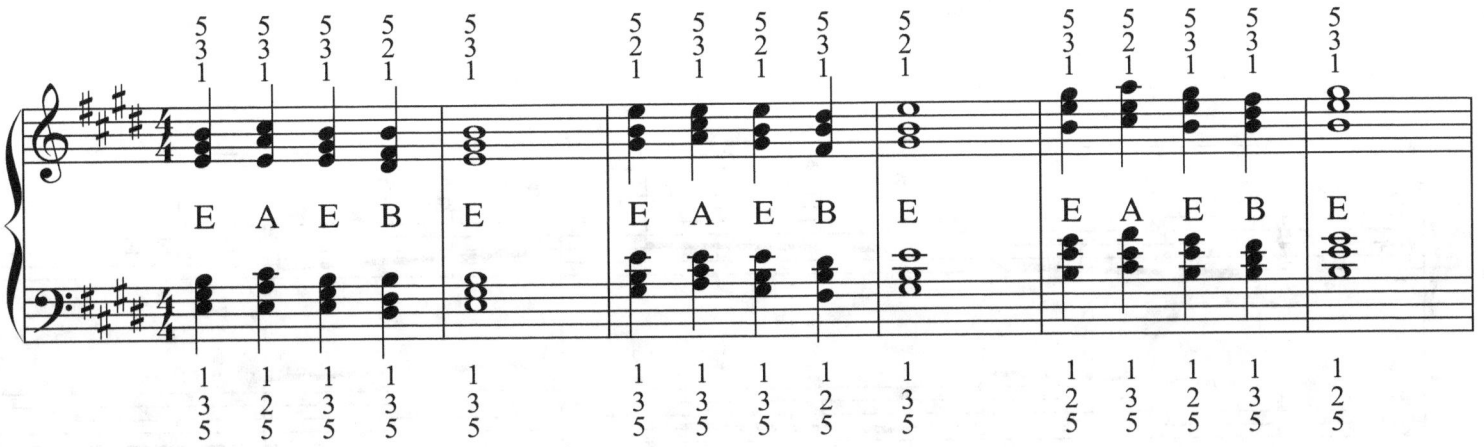

One Octave E Major Arpeggio

Two Octave E Major Arpeggios and Inversions

B Major

Key of B Major
Enharmonically the same as C♭

Five Note Scale

One Octave Scale

Two Octave Scale

Contrary Motion Scale

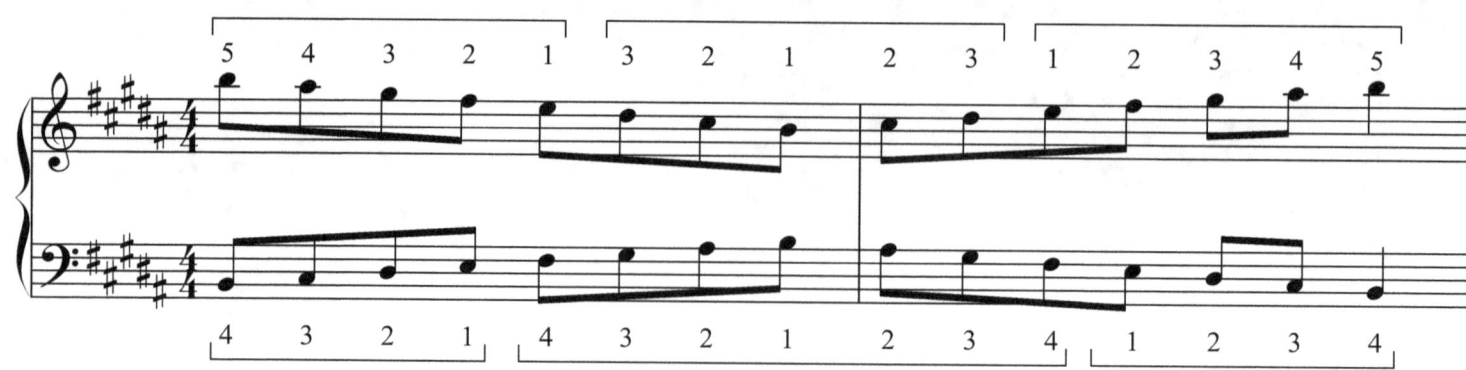

B Major Chord and Inversions

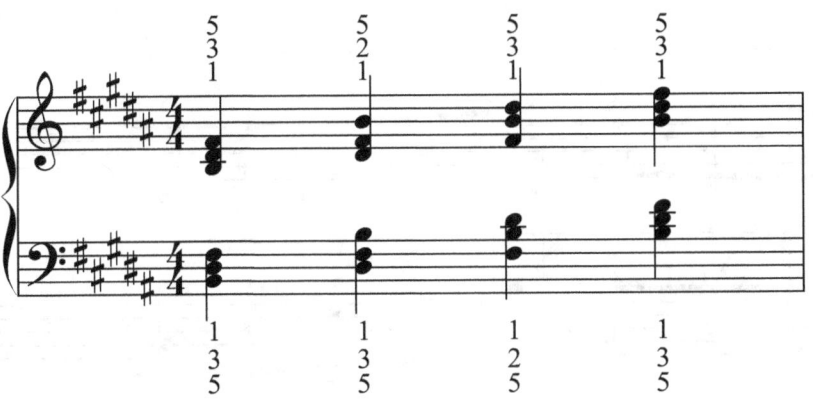

Triads in the Key of B Major

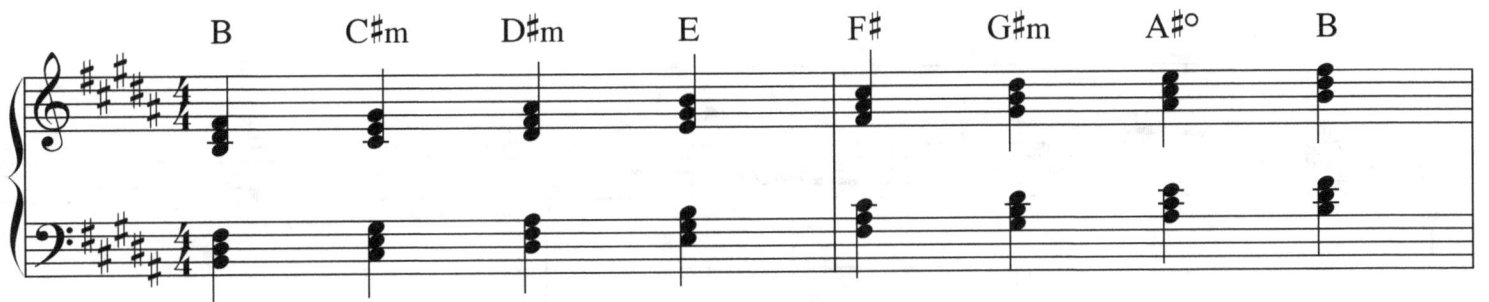

1,4,5 Chord Progression in the Key of B (Cadences)

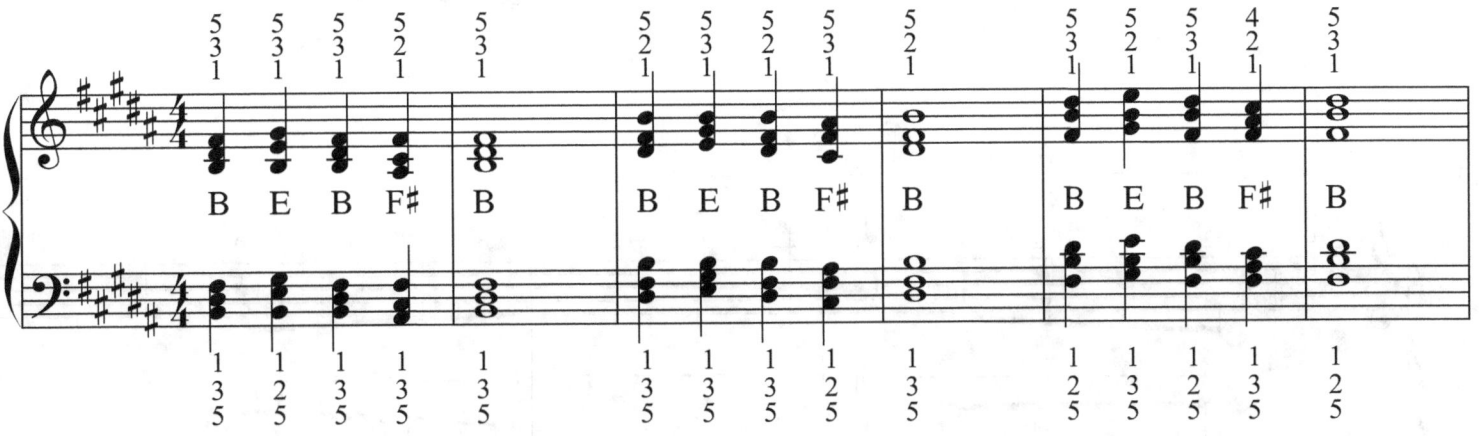

One Octave B Major Arpeggio

Two Octave B Major Arpeggios and Inversions

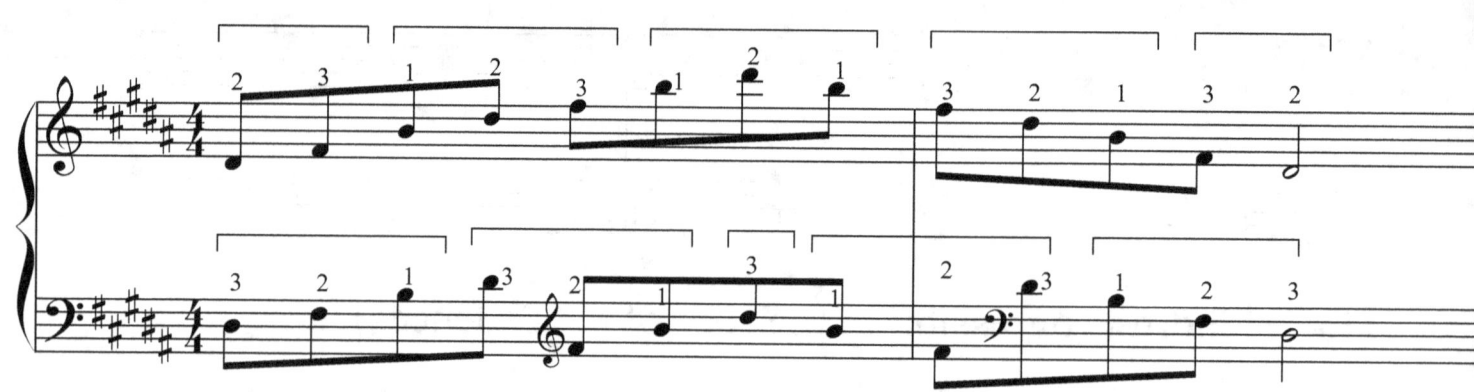

F Major

Key of F Major

Five Note Scale

One Octave Scale

Two Octave Scale

Contrary Motion Scale

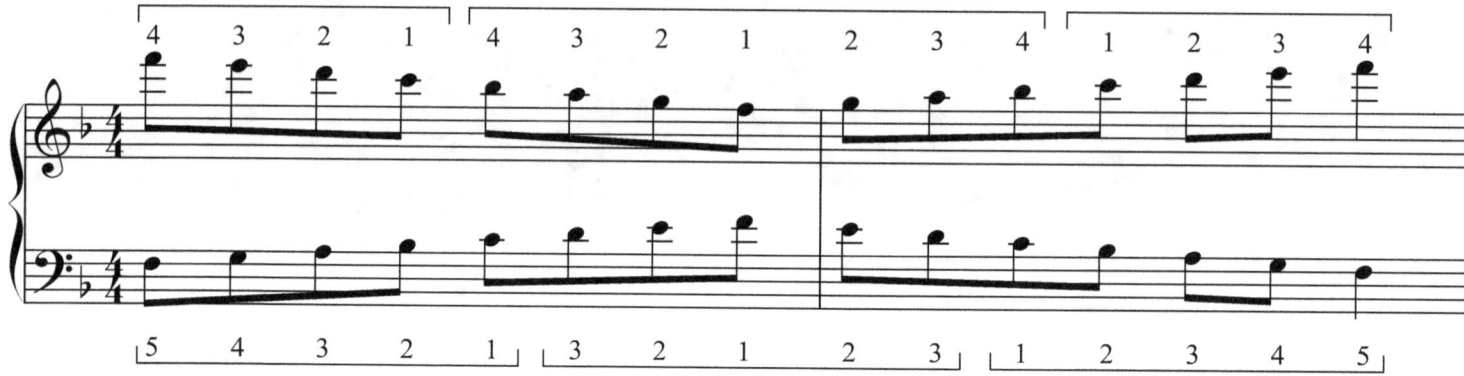

F Major Chord and Inversions

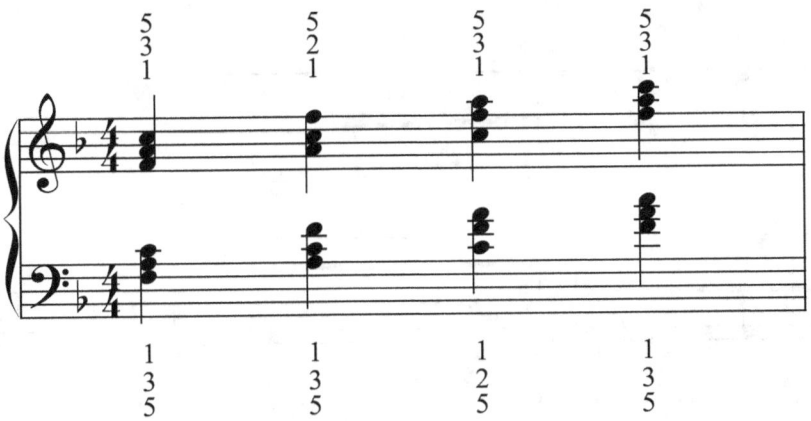

Triads in the Key of F Major

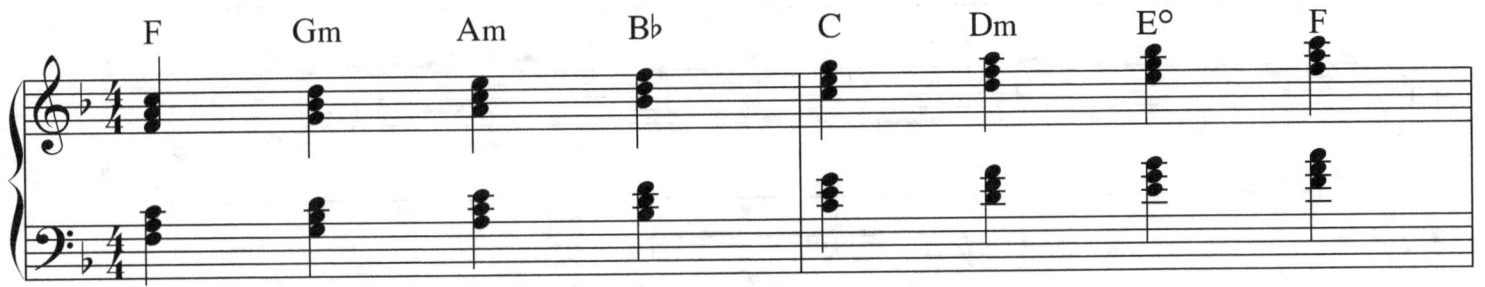

1,4,5 Chord Progression in the Key of F (Cadences)

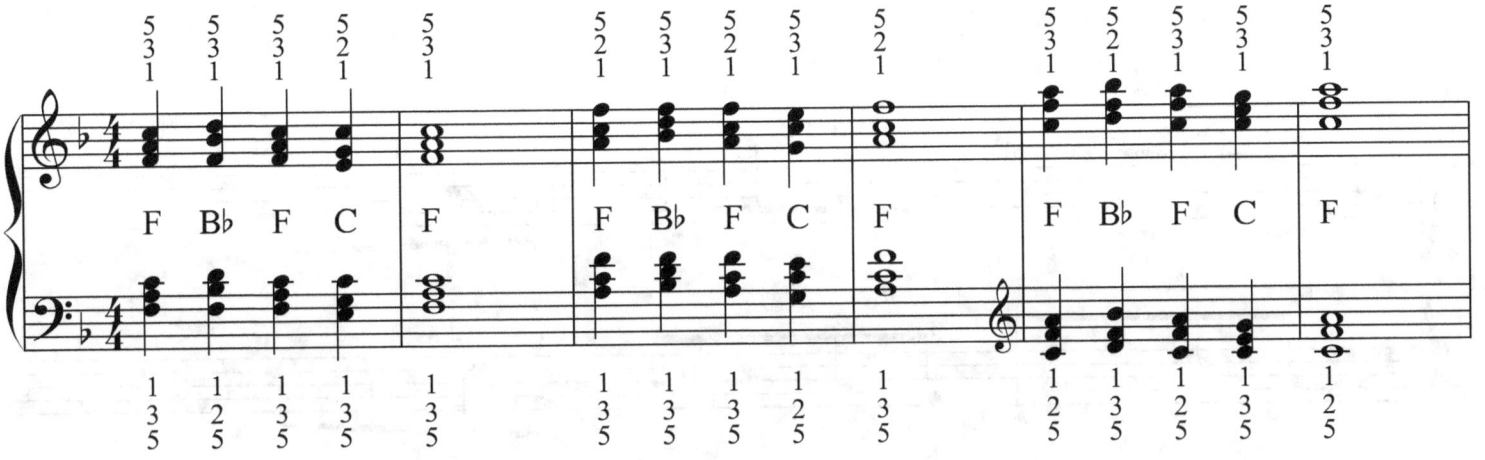

One Octave F Major Arpeggio

Two Octave F Major Arpeggios and Inversions

B♭ Major

Key of B♭ Major
Enharmonically the same as A♯

Five Note Scale

One Octave Scale
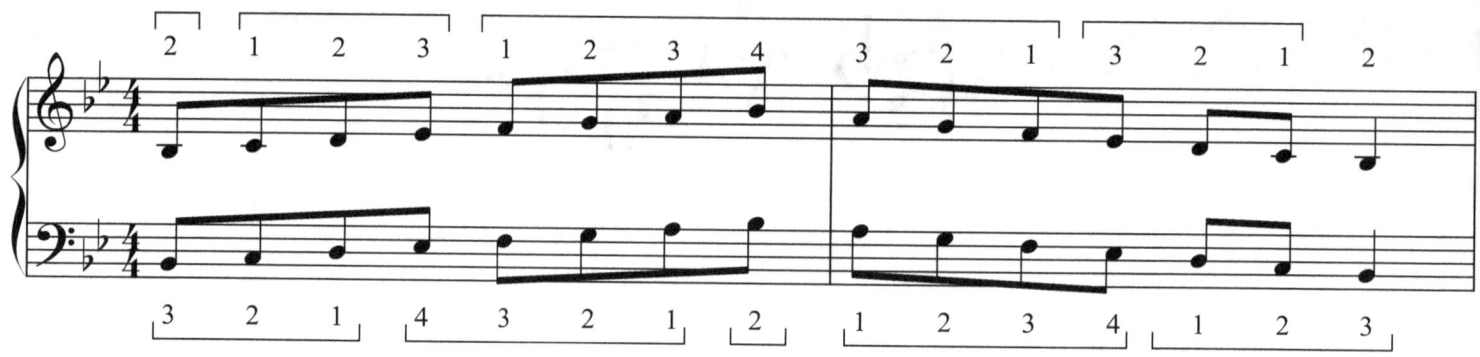

Two Octave Scale
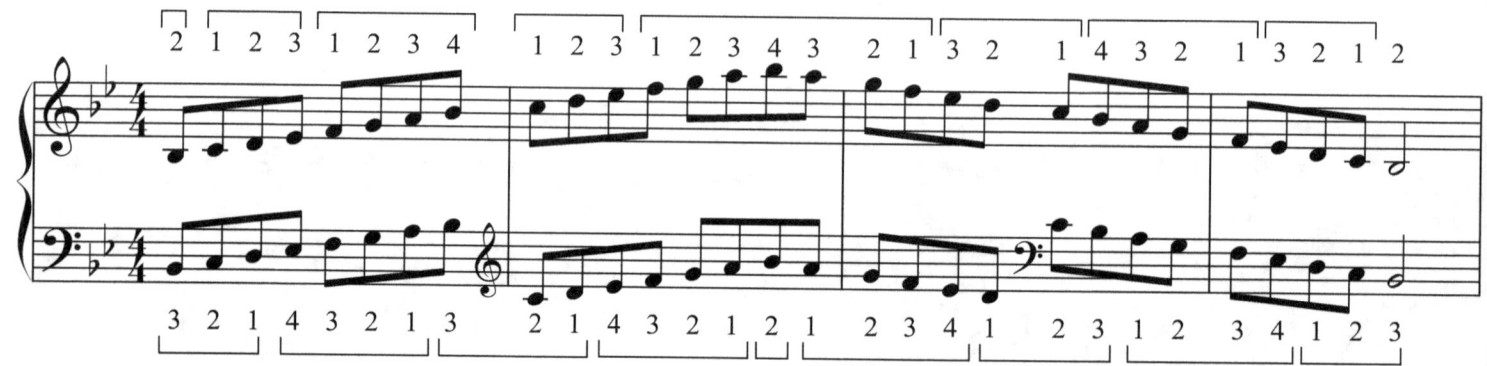

Contrary Motion Scale

B♭ Major Chord and Inversions

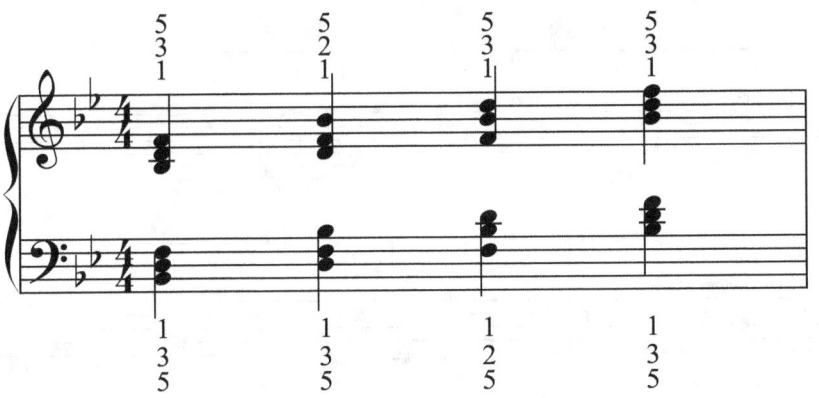

Triads in the Key of B♭ Major

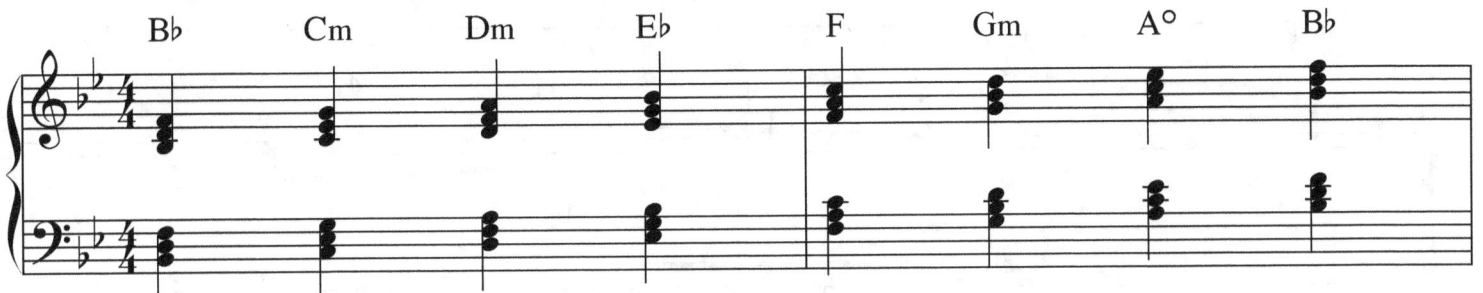

1,4,5 Chord Progression in the Key of B♭ (Cadences)

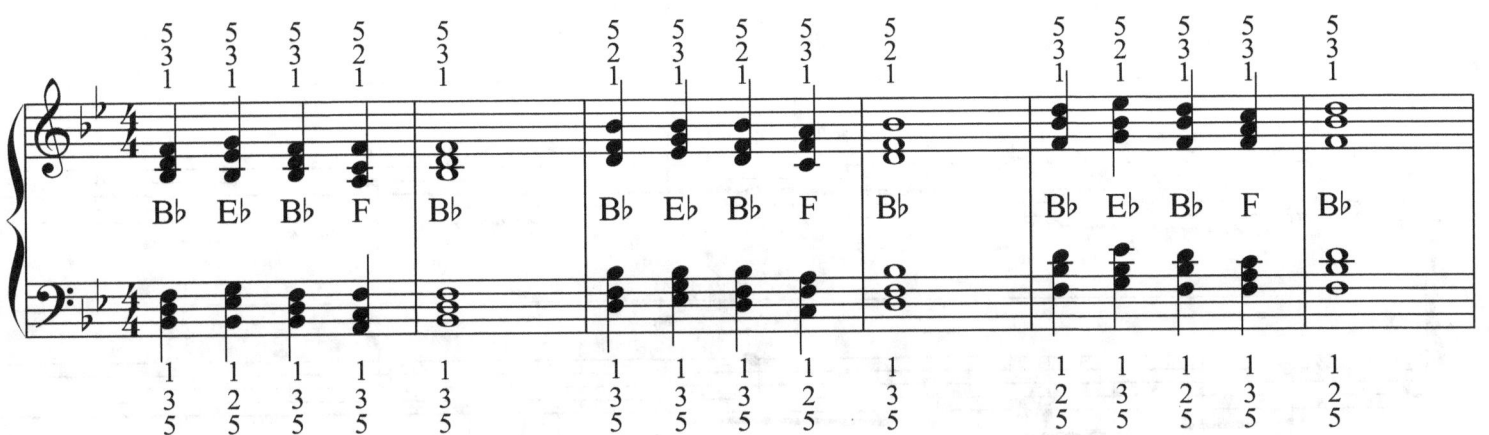

One Octave B♭ Major Arpeggio

Two Octave B♭ Major Arpeggios and Inversions

E♭ Major

Key of E♭ Major
Enharmonically the same as D♯

Five Note Scale
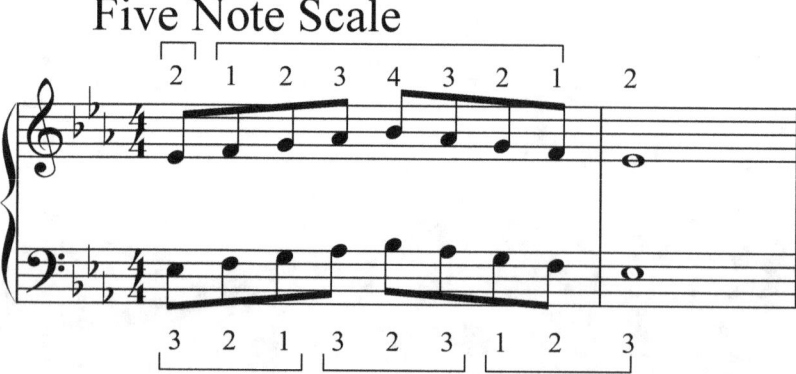

One Octave Scale
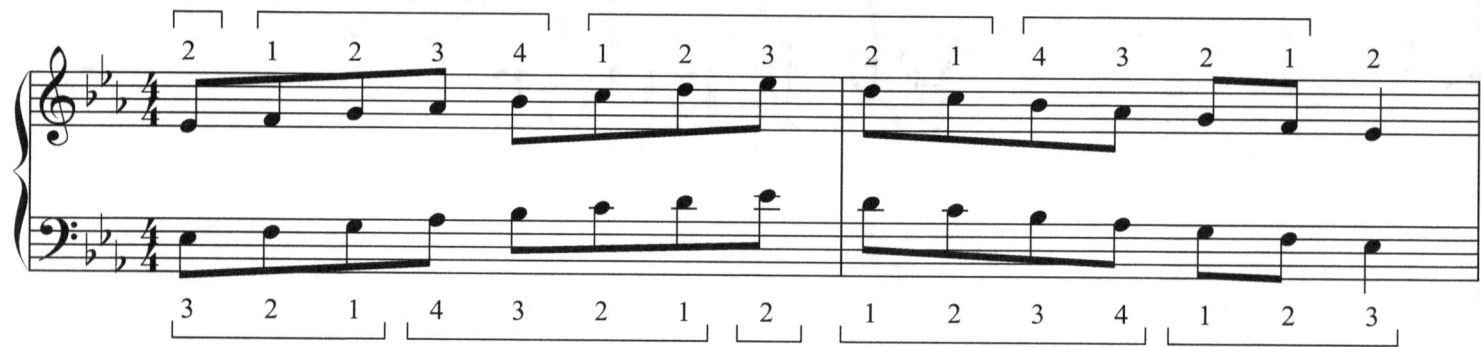

Two Octave Scale

Contrary Motion Scale
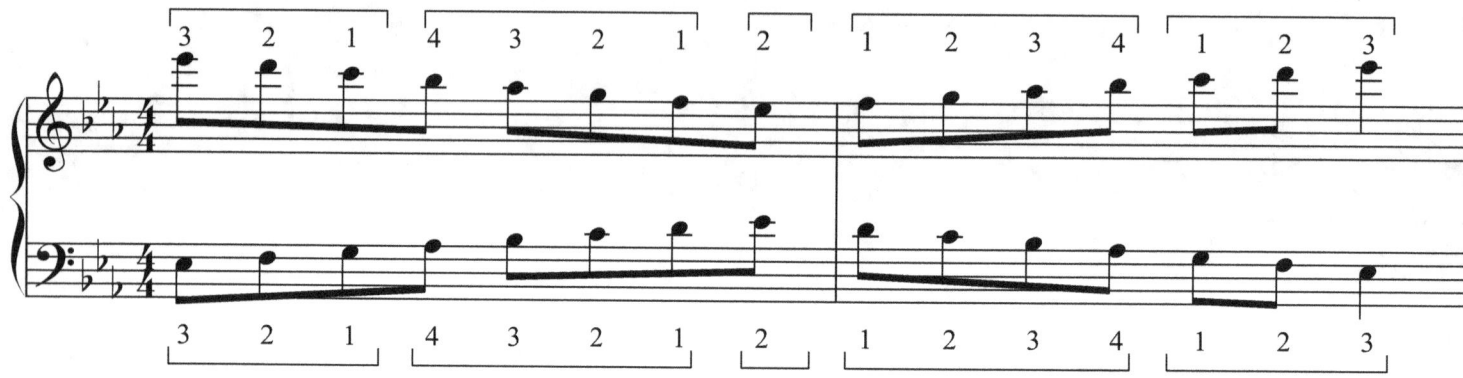

E♭ Major Chord and Inversions

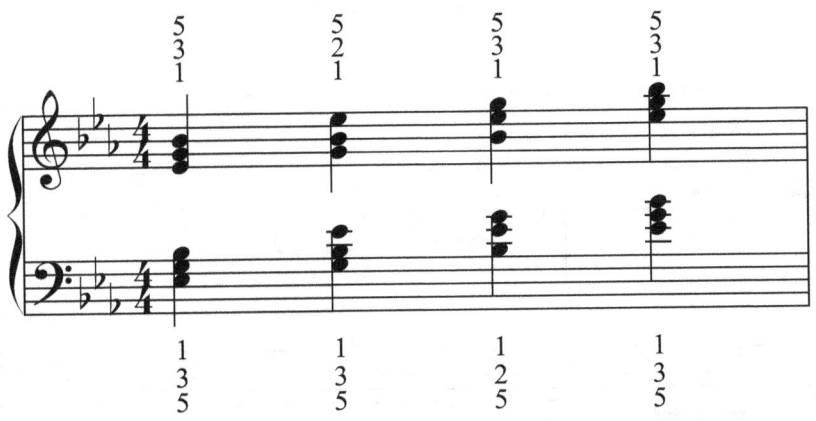

Triads in the Key of E♭ Major

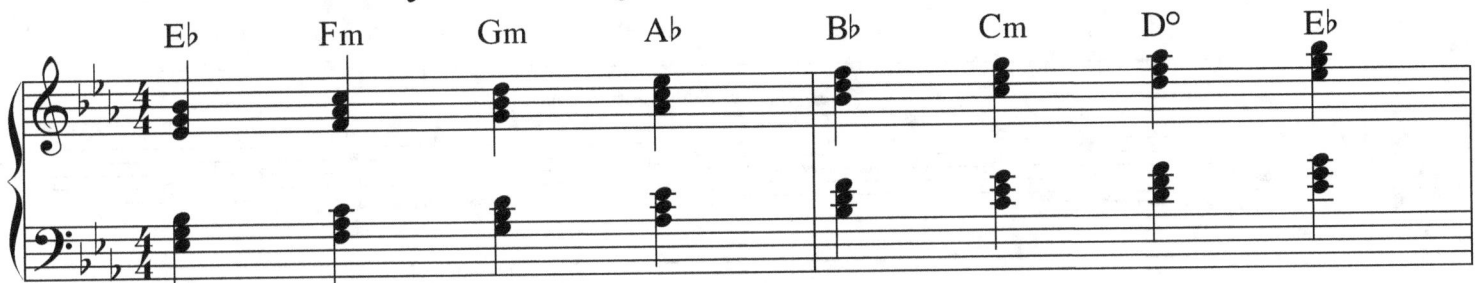

1,4,5 Chord Progression in the Key of E♭ (Cadences)

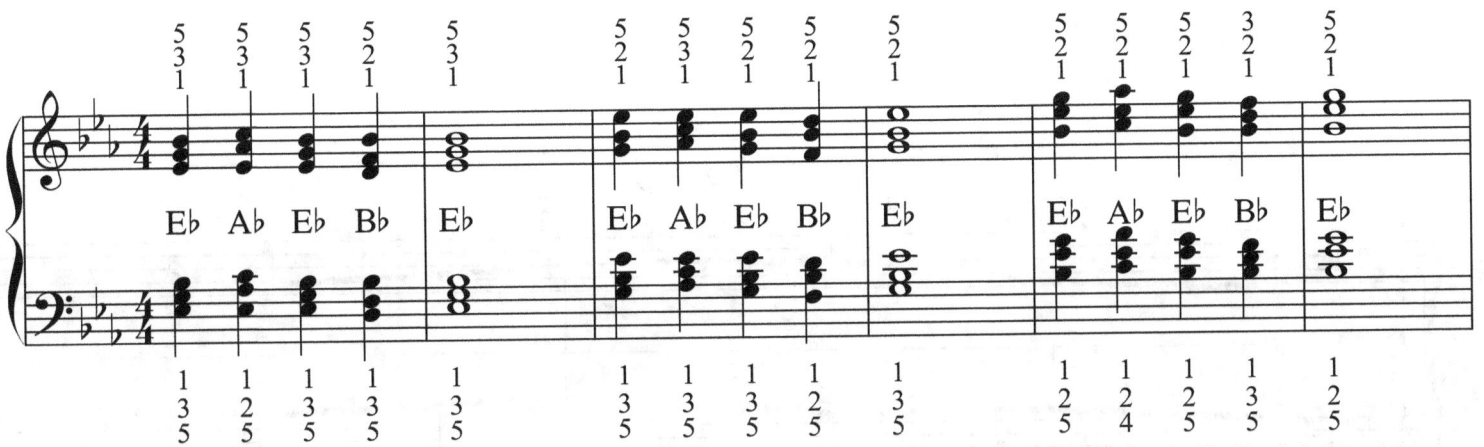

One Octave E♭ Major Arpeggio

Two Octave E♭ Major Arpeggios and Inversions

54

A♭ Major

Key of A♭ Major
Enharmonically the same as G♯

Five Note Scale

One Octave Scale
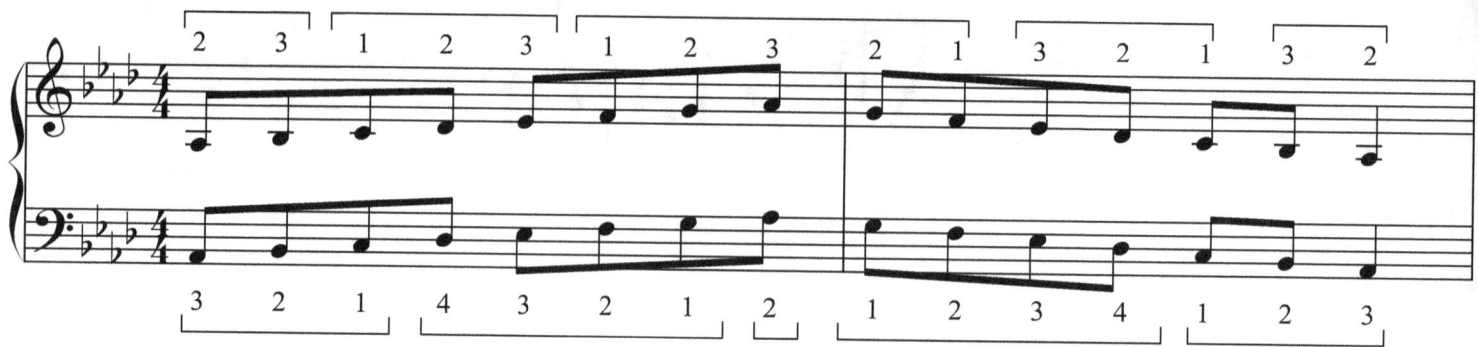

Two Octave Scale

Contrary Motion Scale

A♭ Major Chord and Inversions

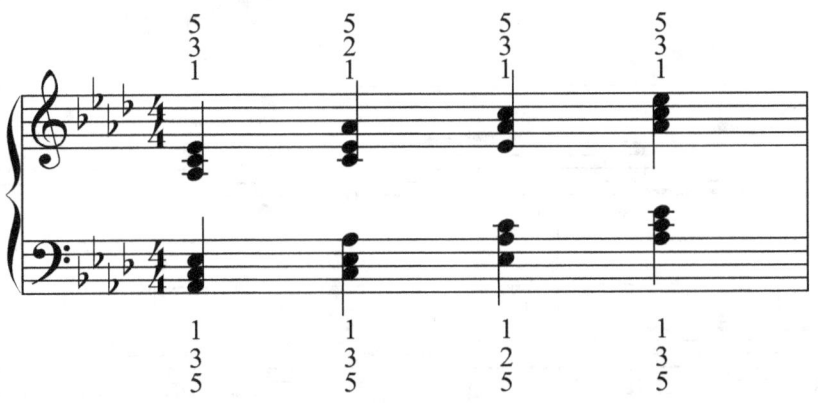

Triads in the Key of A♭ Major

1,4,5 Chord Progression in the Key of A♭ (Cadences)

One Octave A♭ Major Arpeggio

Two Octave A♭ Major Arpeggios and Inversions

D♭ Major

Key of D♭ Major
Enharmonically the same as C♯

Five Note Scale
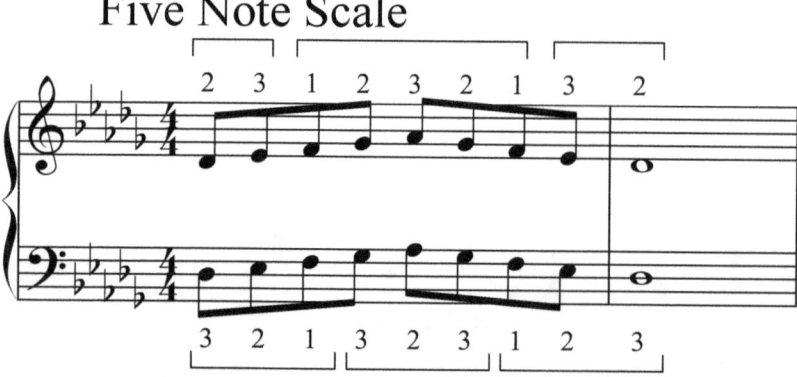

One Octave Scale

Two Octave Scale

Contrary Motion Scale
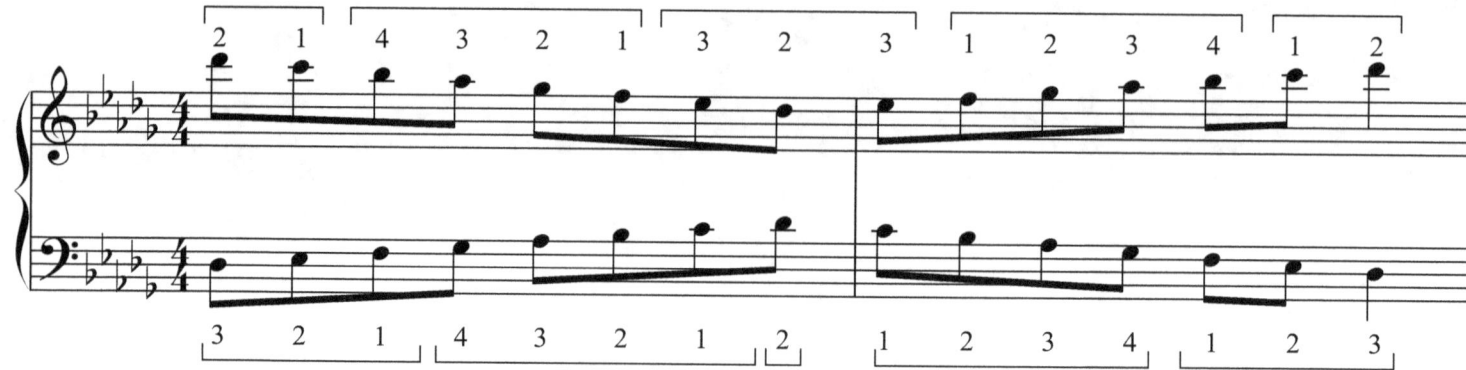

D♭ Major Chord and Inversions

Triads in the Key of D♭ Major

1,4,5 Chord Progression in the Key of D♭ (Cadences)

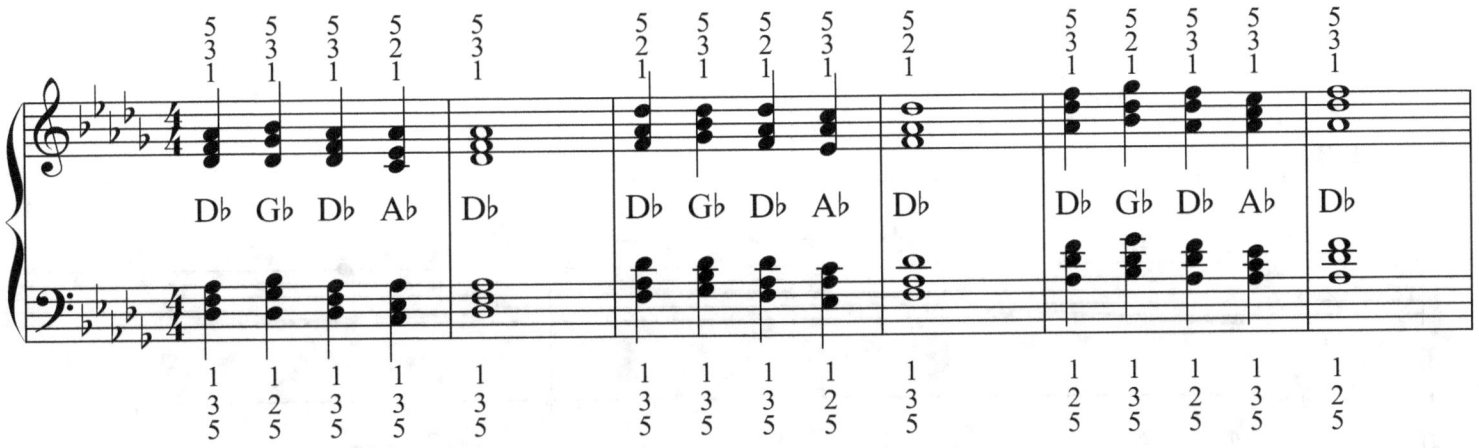

One Octave D♭ Major Arpeggio

Two Octave D♭ Major Arpeggios and Inversions

G♭ Major

Key of G♭ Major
Enharmonically the same as F♯

Five Note Scale

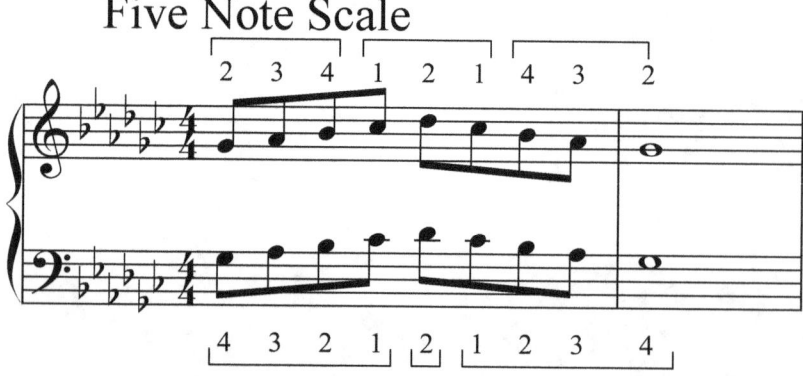

One Octave Scale

Two Octave Scale

Contrary Motion Scale

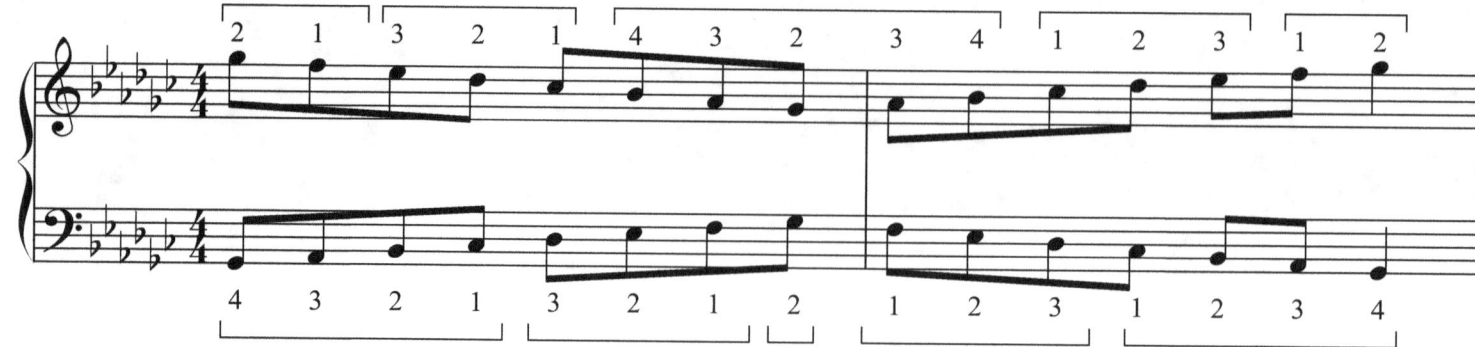

G♭ Major Chord and Inversions

Triads in the Key of G♭ Major

1,4,5 Chord Progression in the Key of G♭ (Cadences)

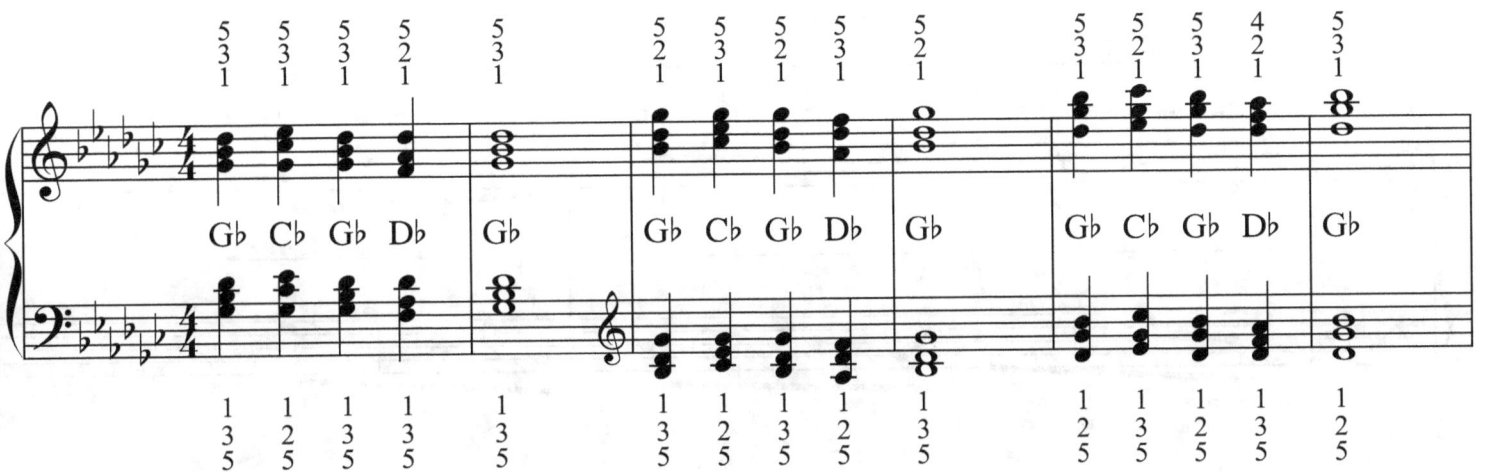

One Octave G♭ Major Arpeggio

Two Octave G♭ Major Arpeggios and Inversions

66

Major Cadences with Dominant 7th Chord

Note - The Major Cadences are presented in order of the number of sharps and flats in the key (C no sharps, G 1 sharp, D 2 sharps, etc.).

Minor Keys

A Minor

A Minor 72
E Minor 75
B Minor 79
F♯ Minor 83
C♯ Minor 87
G♯ Minor 91
D Minor 95
G Minor 99
C Minor 103
C Minor 103
F Minor 107
B♭ Minor 111

Note - The Minor keys are presented in order of the number of sharps and flats in the key (Am no sharps, Em 1 sharp, Bm 2 sharps, etc.).

Key of A Minor

Five Note Scale

One Octave Scale

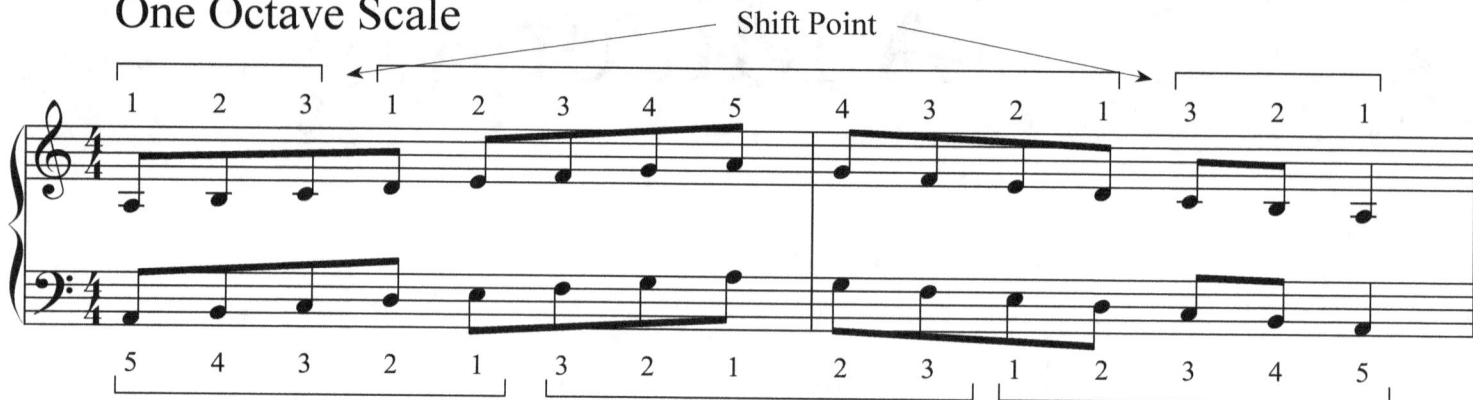

Two Octave Scale

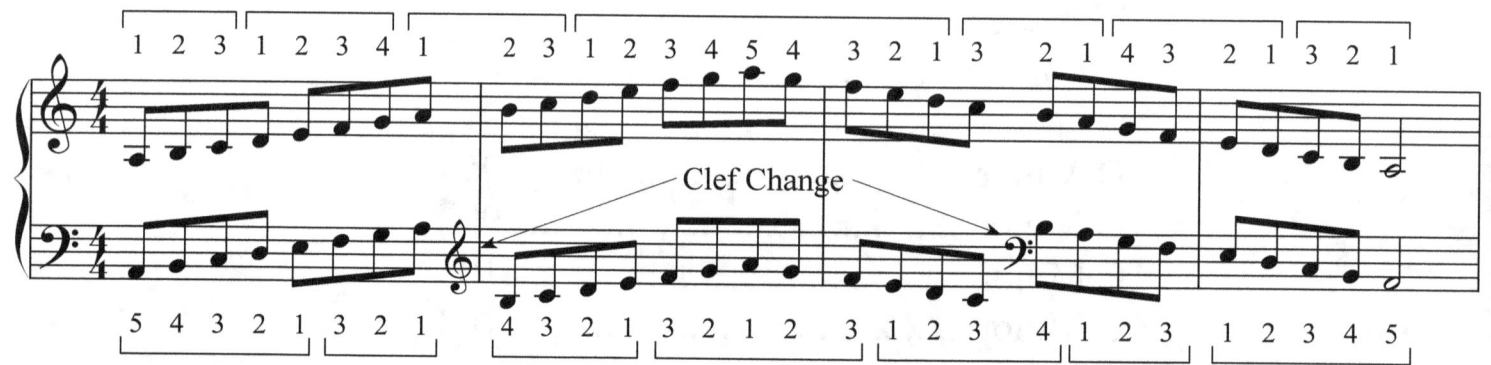

Contrary Motion Scale

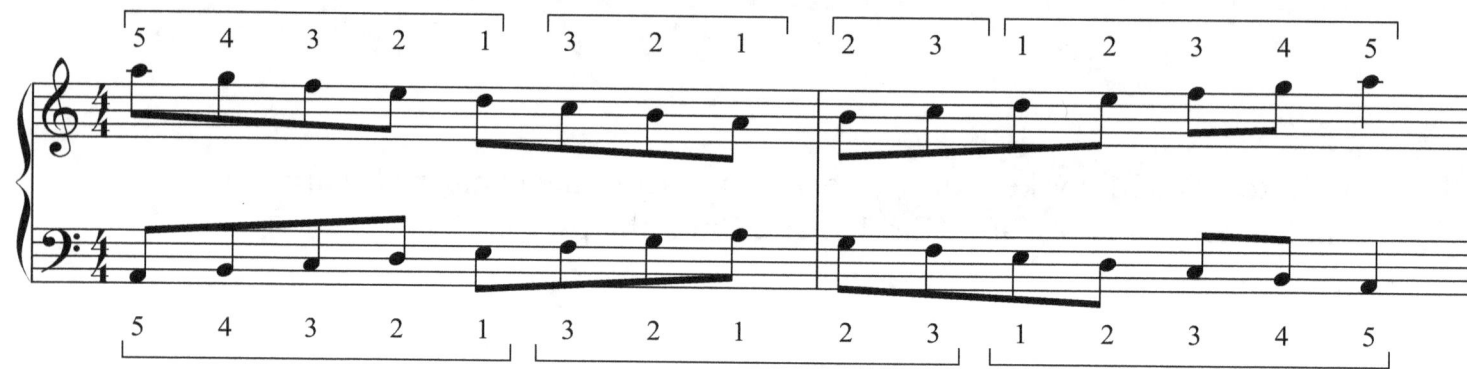

A minor Chord and Inversions

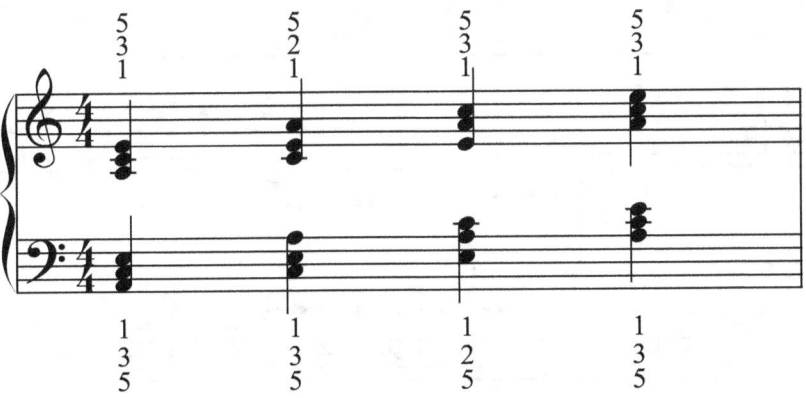

Triads in the Key of A minor

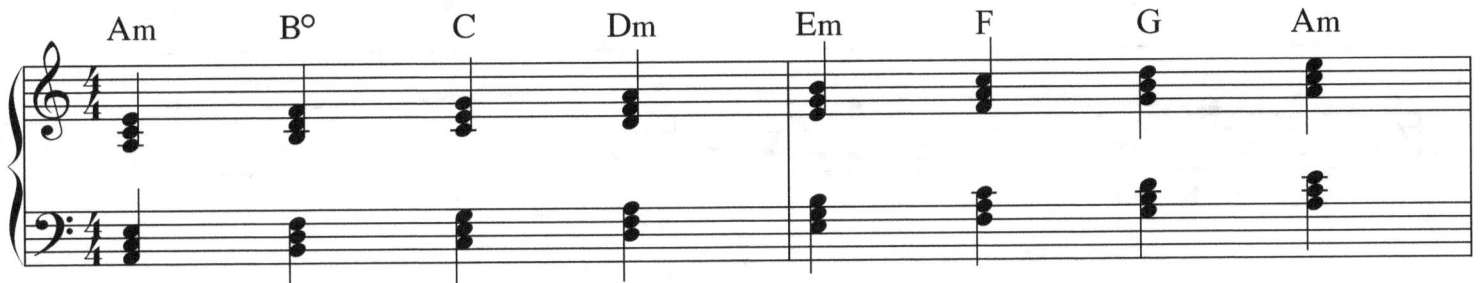

1,4,5 Chord Progression in the Key of A Minor (cadences)

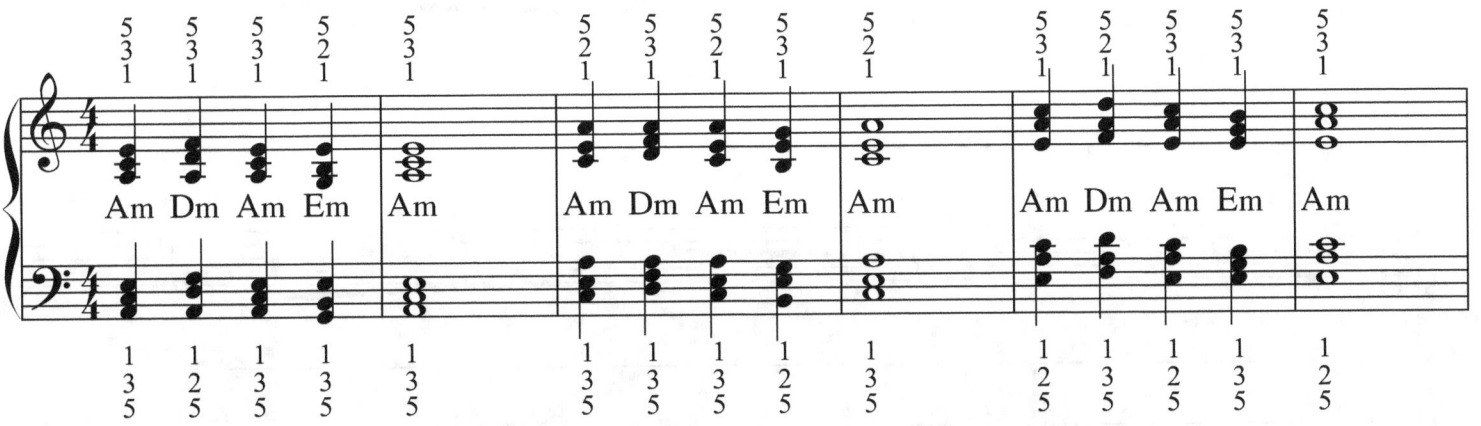

One Octave A Minor Arpeggio

Two Octave A Minor Arpeggios and Inversions

Remember that fingerings are suggestions and not rules. Practicing with consistent fingerings will help you memorize the scales and develop muscle memory.

E Minor

Key of E Minor

Five Note Scale

One Octave Scale

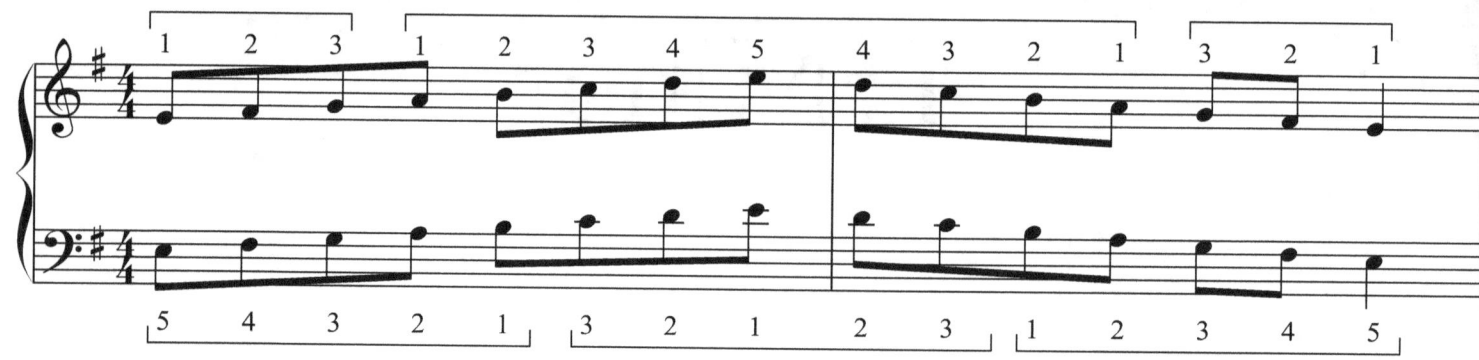

Two Octave Scale

Contrary Motion Scale

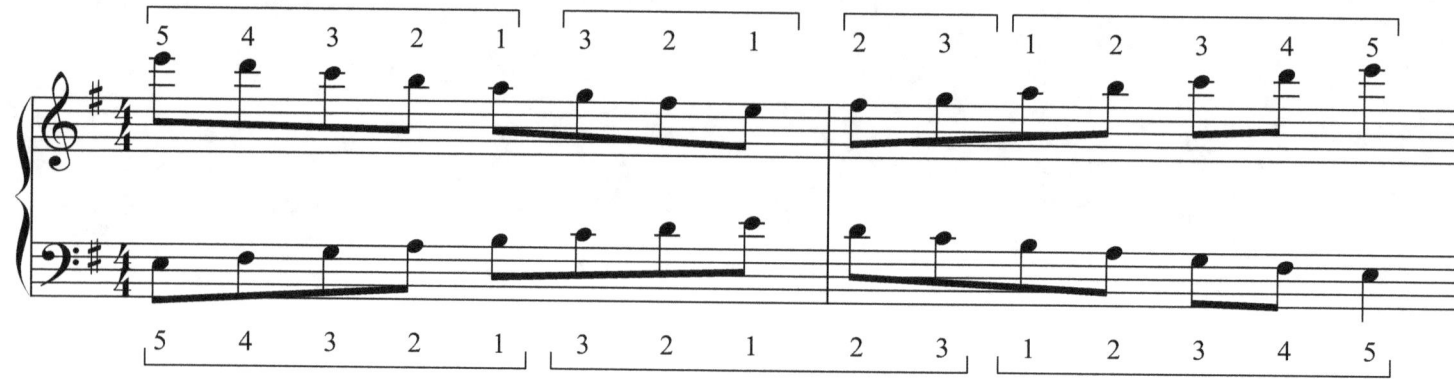

E minor Chord and Inversions

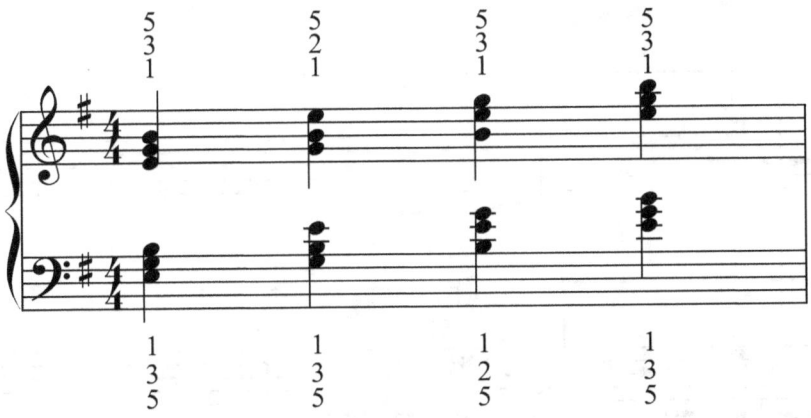

Triads in the Key of E minor

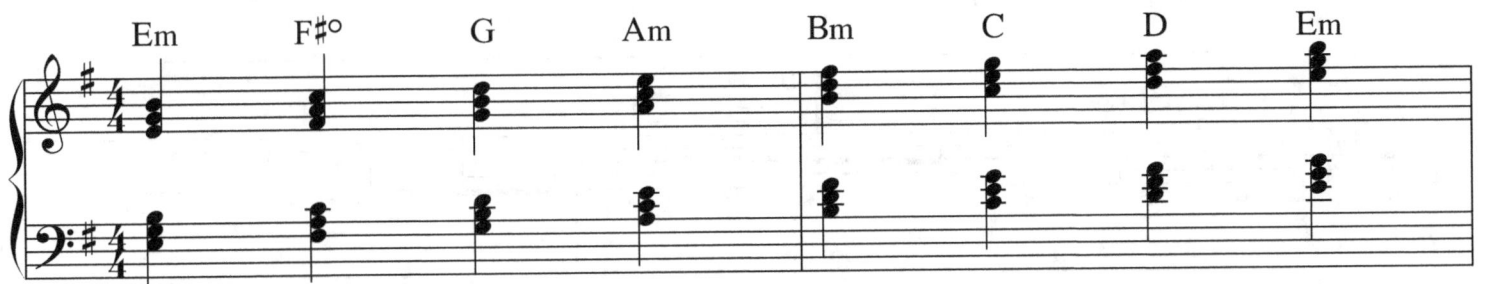

1,4,5 Chord Progression in the Key of E Minor (cadences)

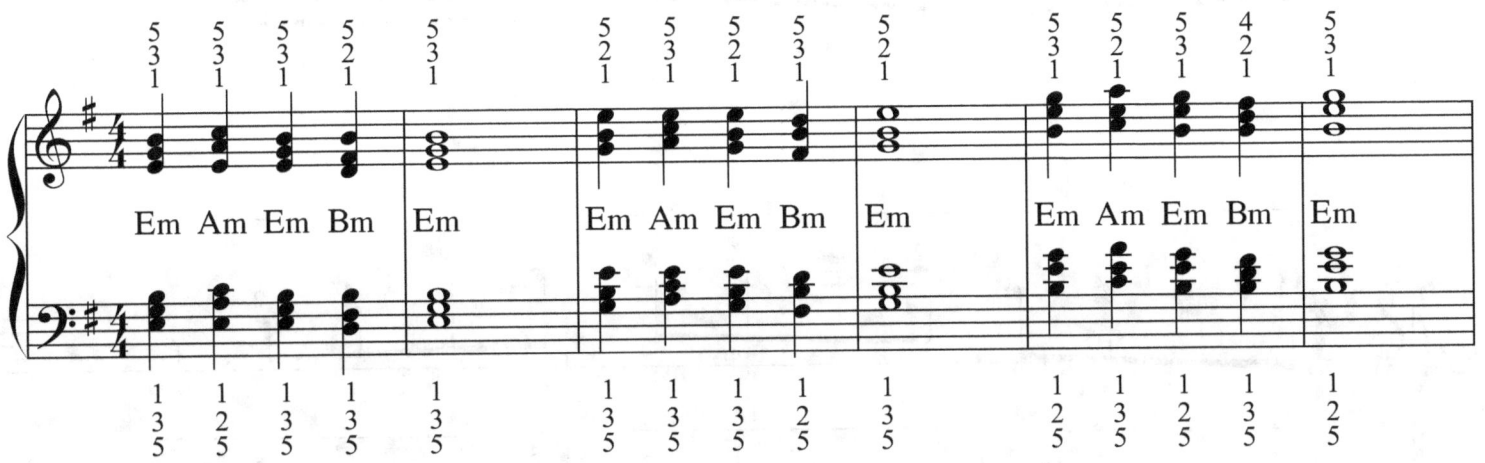

One Octave E Minor Arpeggio

Two Octave E Minor Arpeggios and Inversions

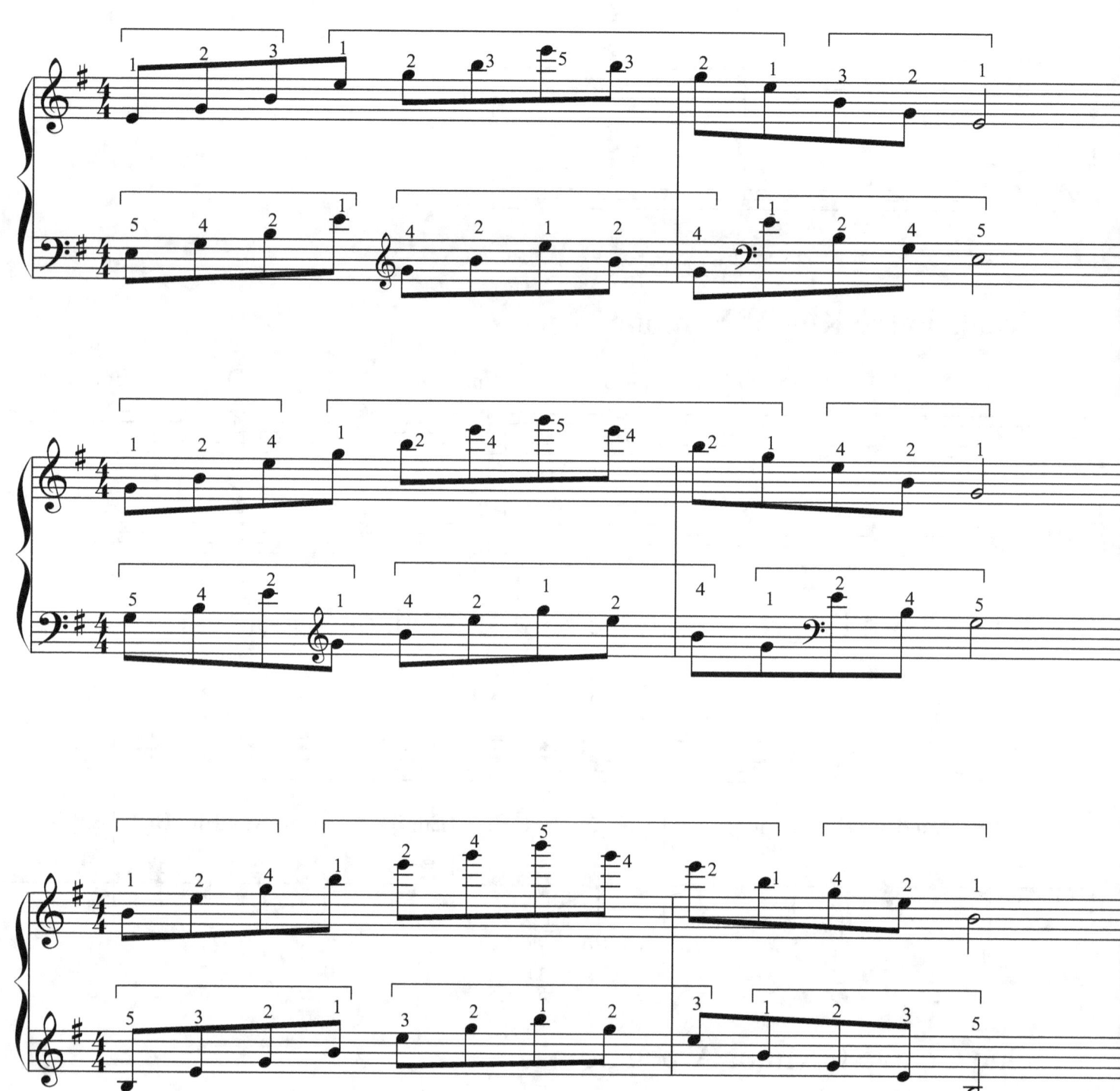

78

B Minor

Key of B Minor

Five Note Scale
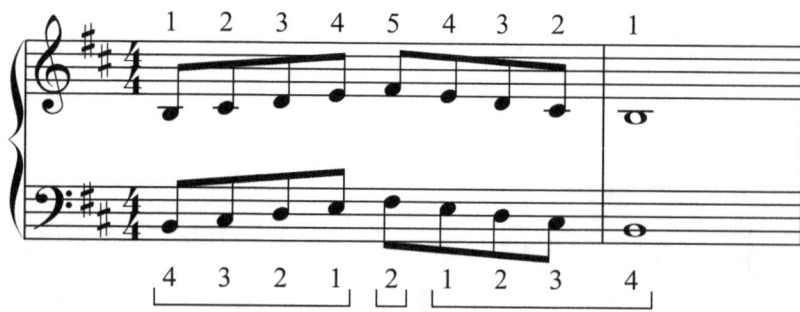

One Octave Scale
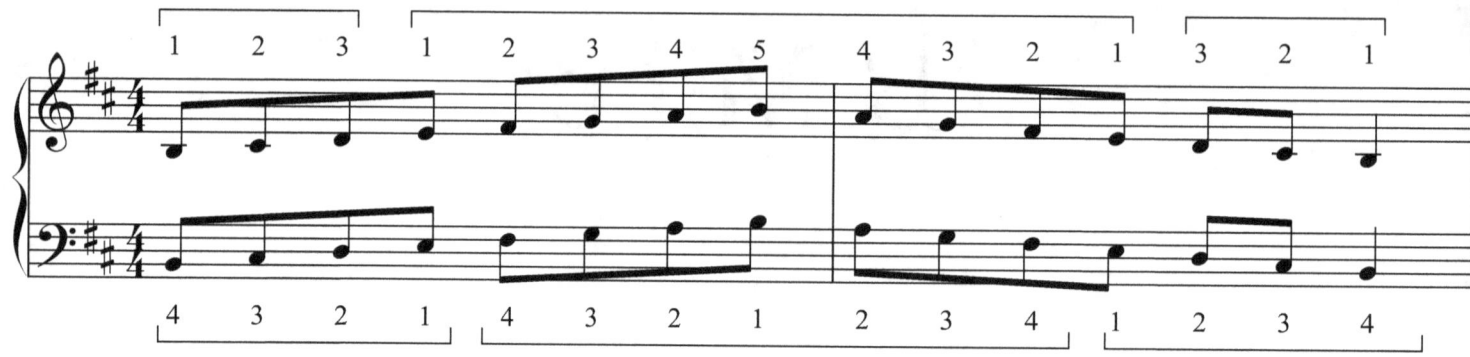

Two Octave Scale
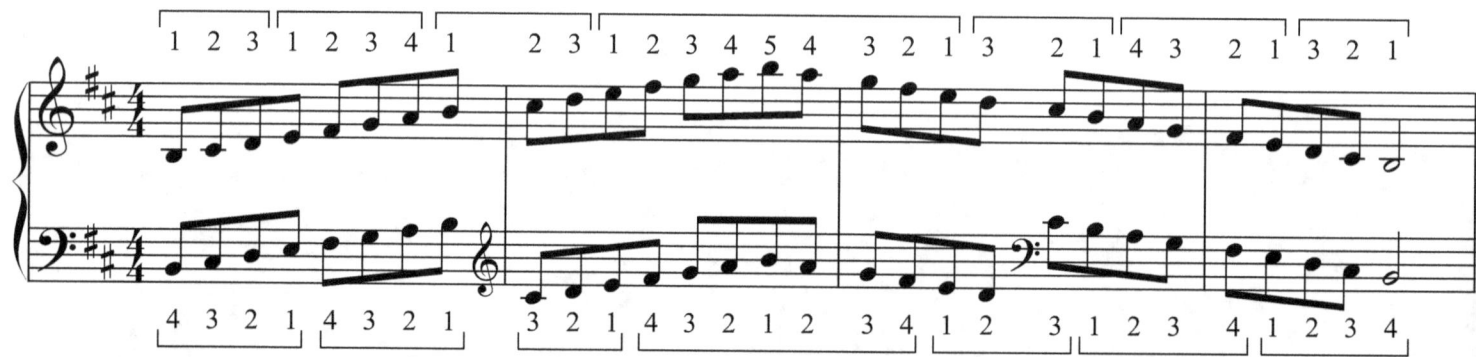

Contrary Motion Scale
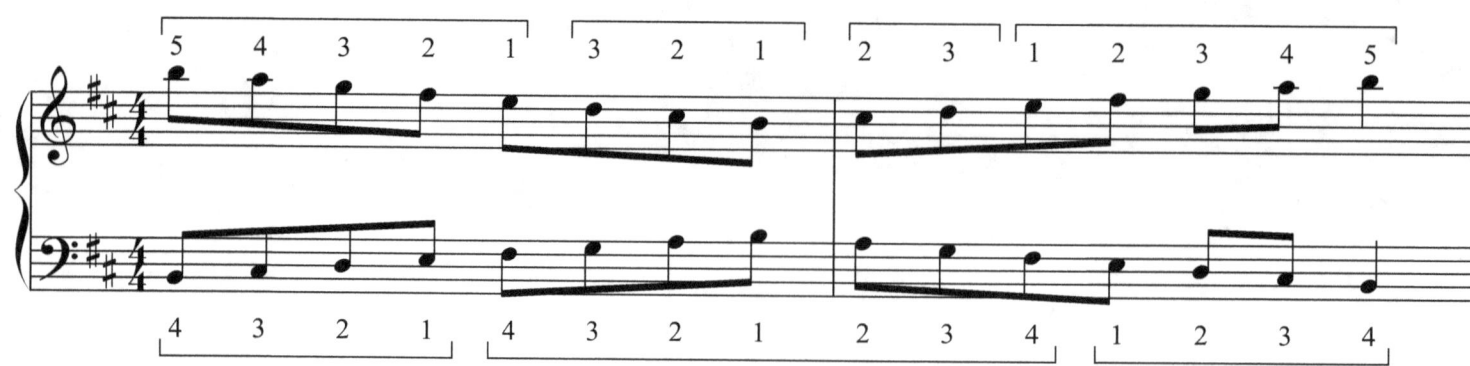

B minor Chord and Inversions

Triads in the Key of B minor

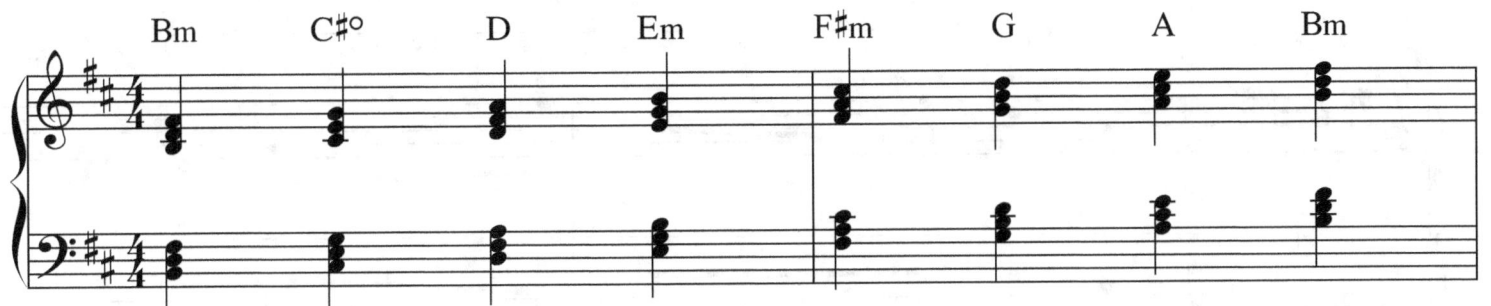

1,4,5 Chord Progression in the Key of B Minor (cadences)

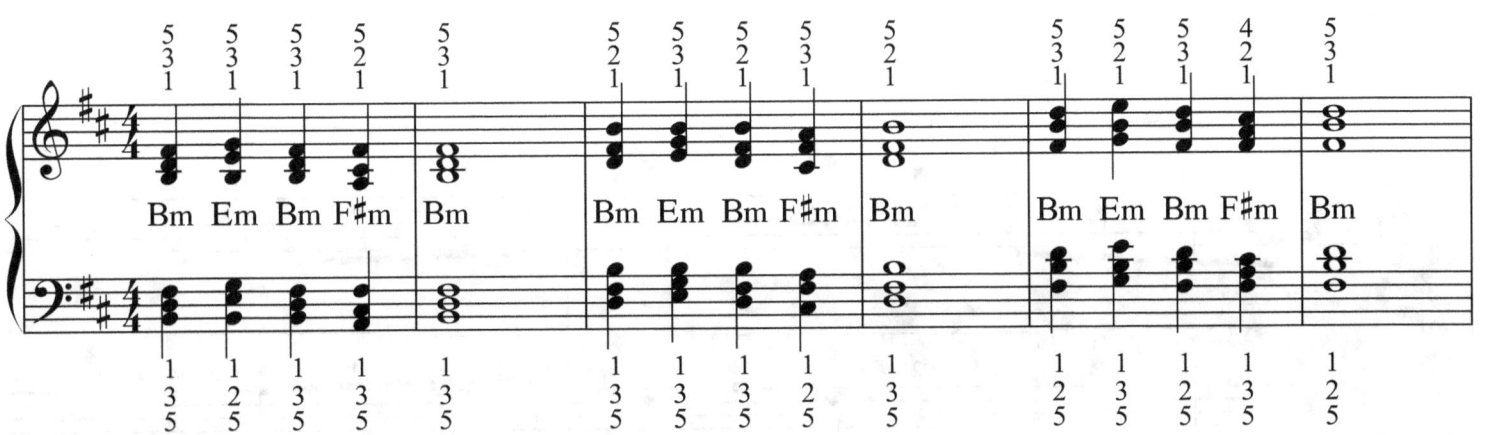

One Octave B Minor Arpeggio

Two Octave B Minor Arpeggios and Inversions

F# Minor

Key of F# Minor
Enharmonically the same as G♭

Five Note Scale
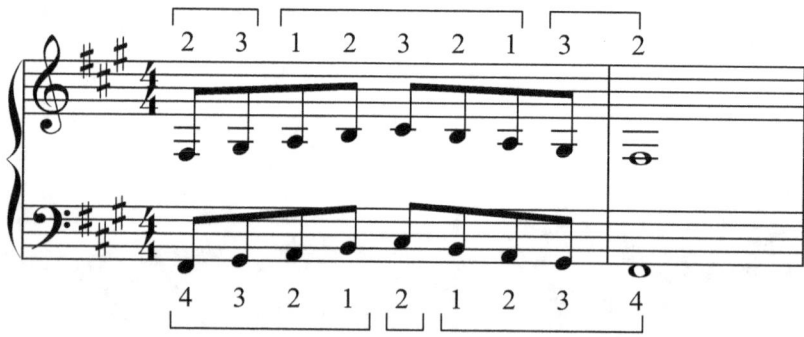

One Octave Scale

Two Octave Scale

Contrary Motion Scale

F# minor Chord and Inversions

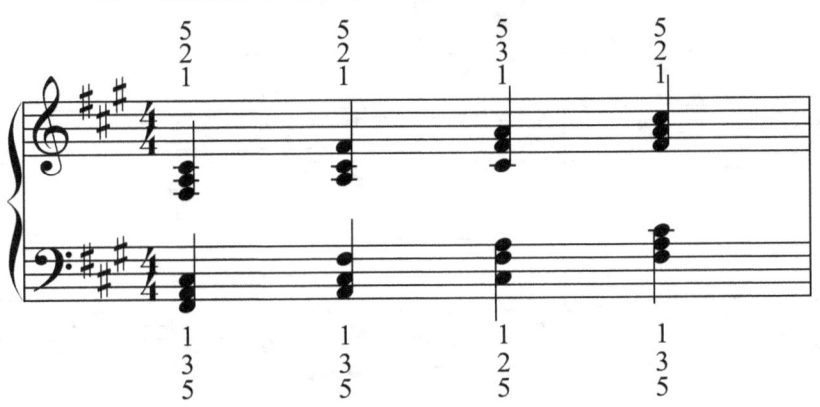

Triads in the Key of F# minor

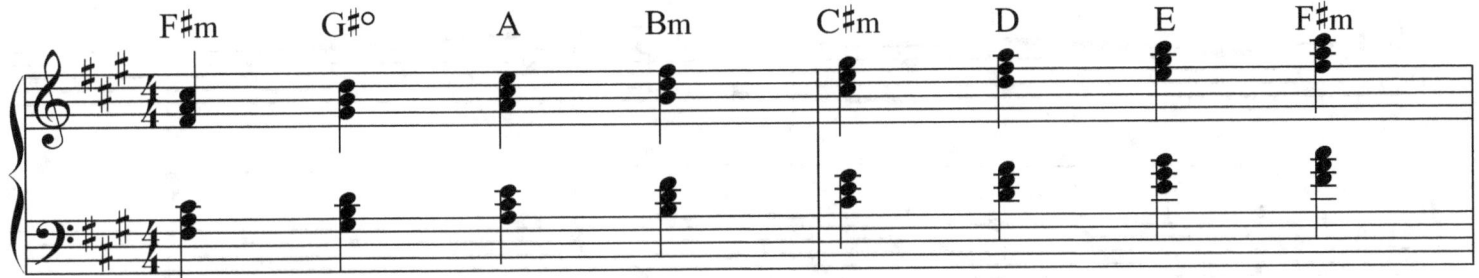

1,4,5 Chord Progression in the Key of F# Minor (cadences)

One Octave F# Minor Arpeggio

Two Octave F# Minor Arpeggios and Inversions

C♯ Minor

Key of C# Minor
Enharmonically the same as D♭

Five Note Scale

One Octave Scale

Two Octave Scale

Contrary Motion Scale

C♯ minor Chord and Inversions

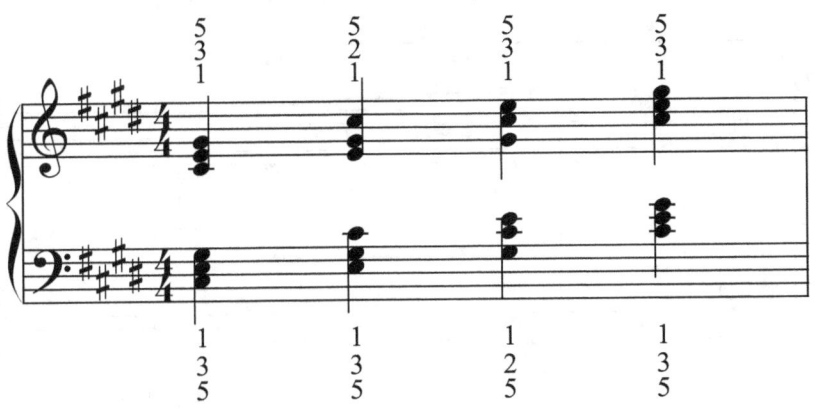

Triads in the Key of C♯ minor

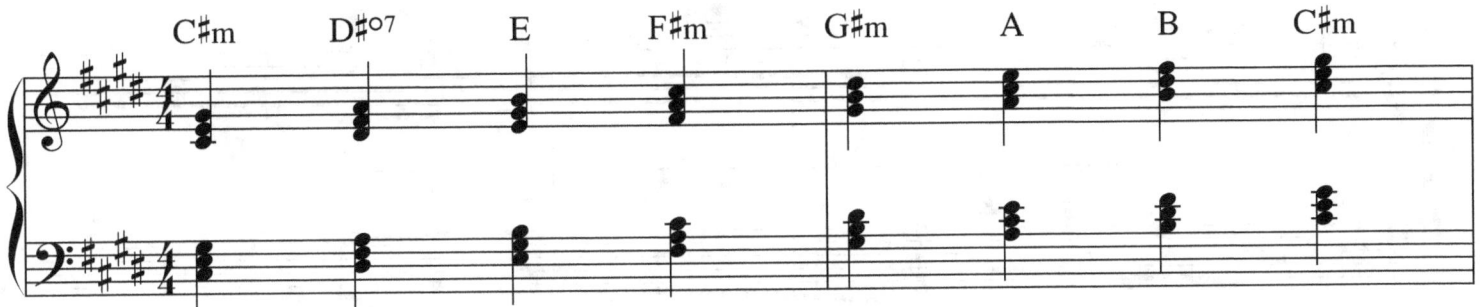

1,4,5 Chord Progression in the Key of C♯ Minor (cadences)

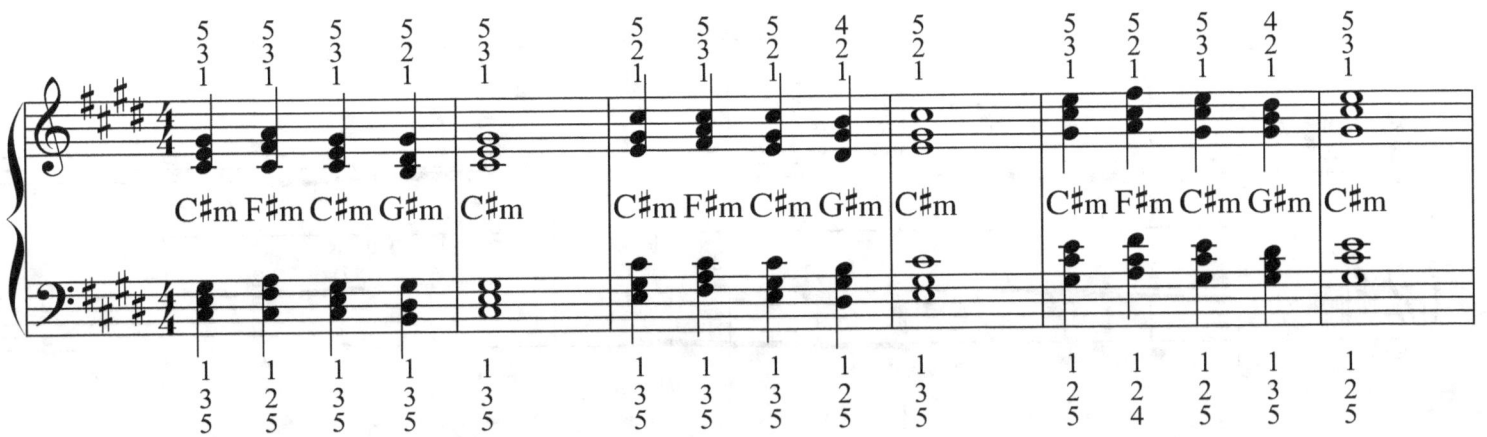

One Octave C♯ Minor Arpeggio

Two Octave C# Minor Arpeggios and Inversions

G♯ Minor

Key of G# Minor
Enharmonically the same as A♭

Five Note Scale
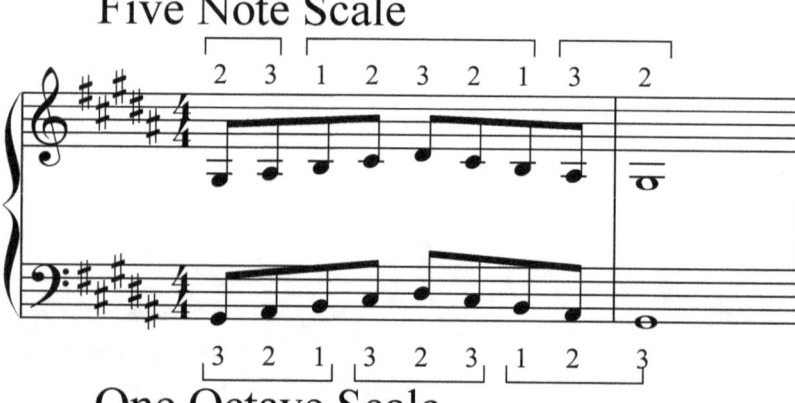

One Octave Scale
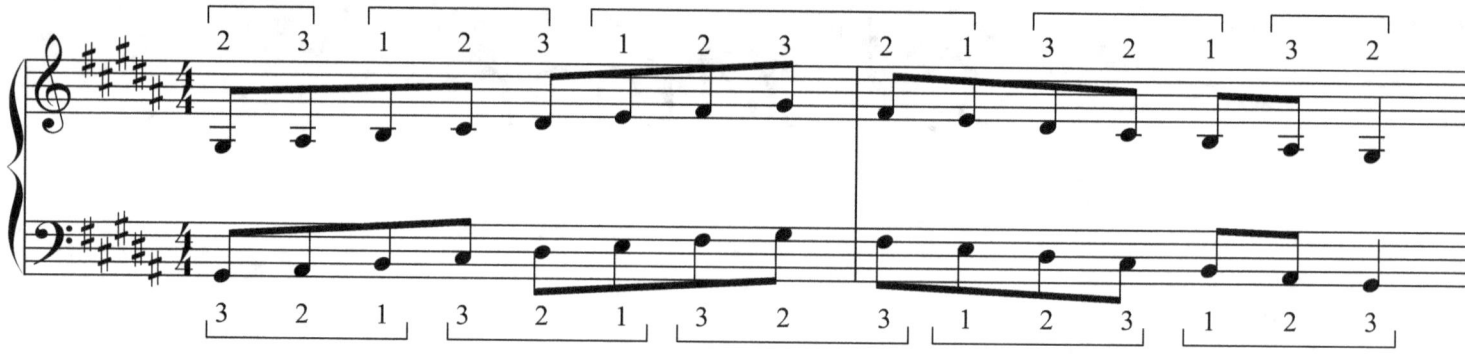

Two Octave Scale

Contrary Motion Scale
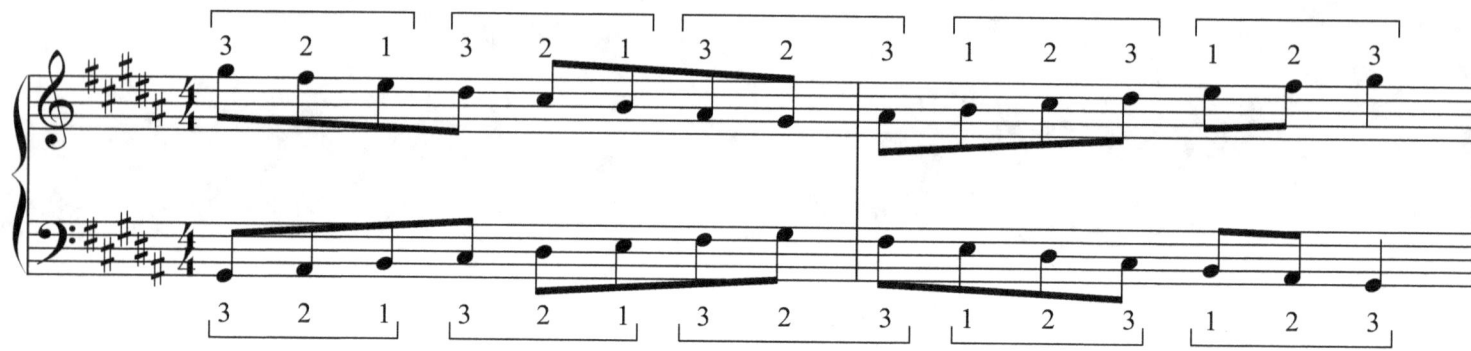

G# minor Chord and Inversions

Triads in the Key of G# minor

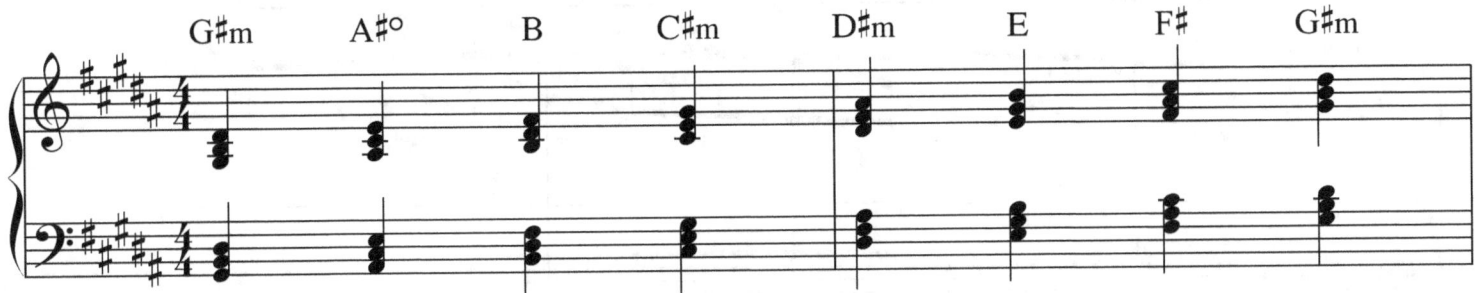

1,4,5 Chord Progression in the Key of G# Minor (cadences)

One Octave G# Minor Arpeggio

Two Octave G# Minor Arpeggios and Inversions

D Minor

Key of D Minor

Five Note Scale

One Octave Scale

Two Octave Scale

Contrary Motion Scale

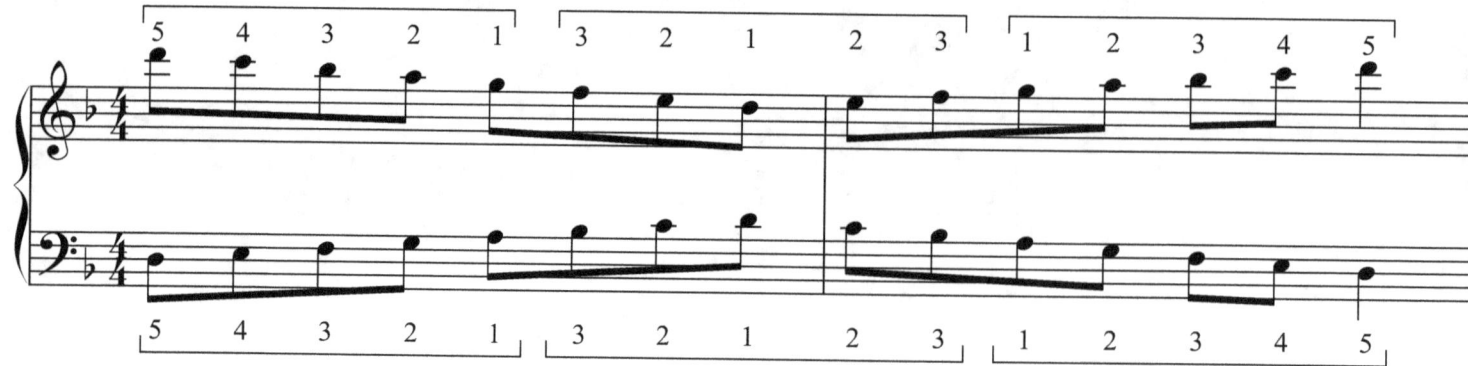

D minor Chord and Inversions

Triads in the Key of D minor

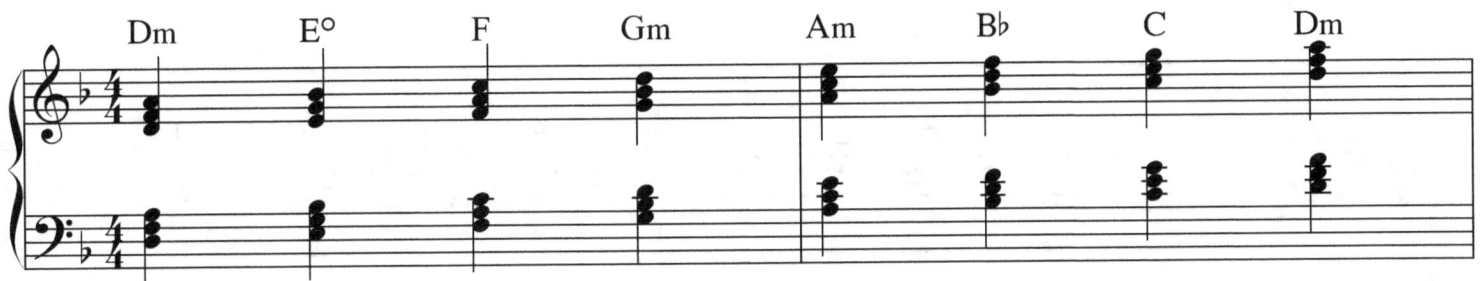

1,4,5 Chord Progression in the Key of D Minor (cadences)

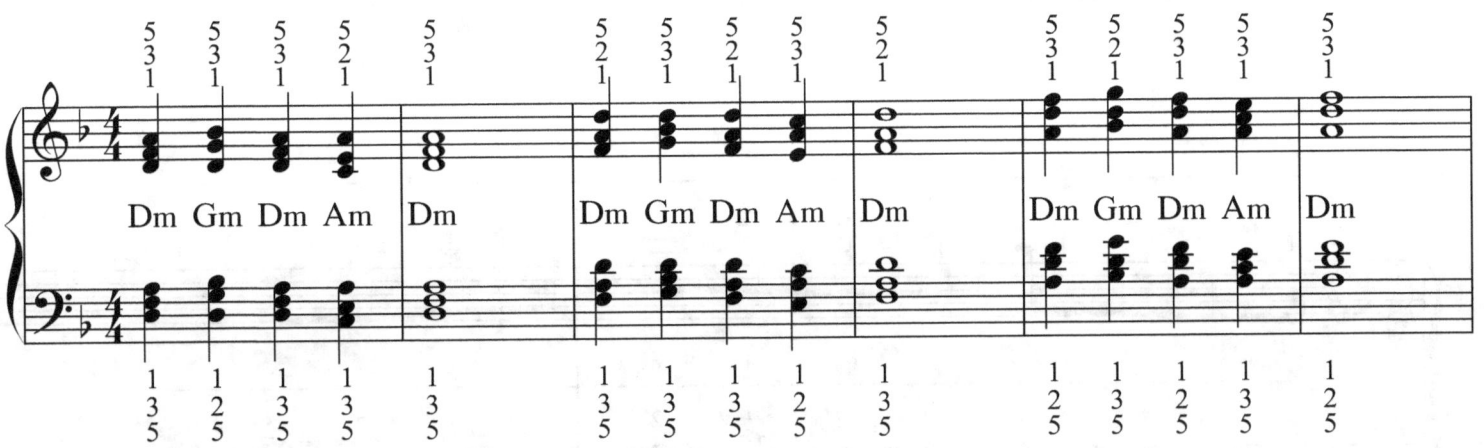

One Octave D Minor Arpeggio

Two Octave D Minor Arpeggios and Inversions

98

G Minor

Key of G Minor

Five Note Scale

One Octave Scale

Two Octave Scale

Contrary Motion Scale

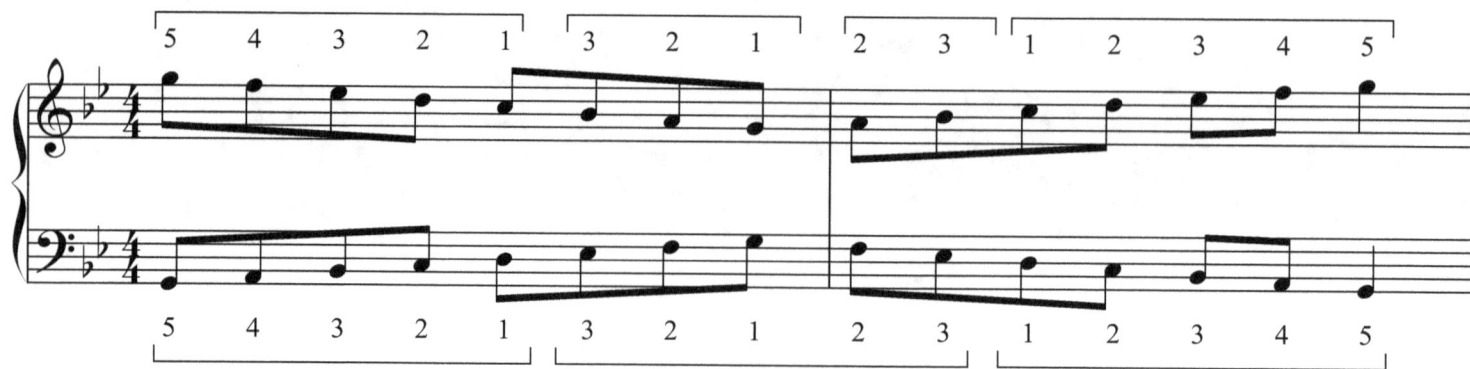

G minor Chord and Inversions

Triads in the Key of G minor

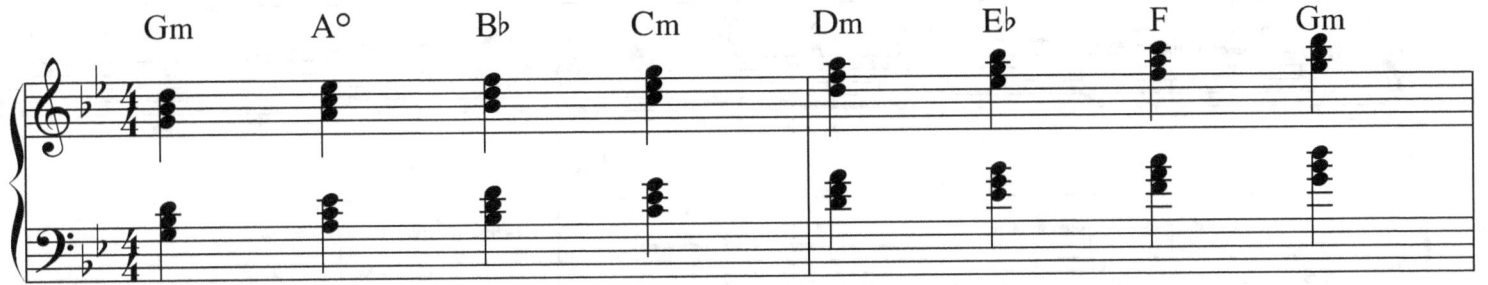

1,4,5 Chord Progression in the Key of G Minor (cadences)

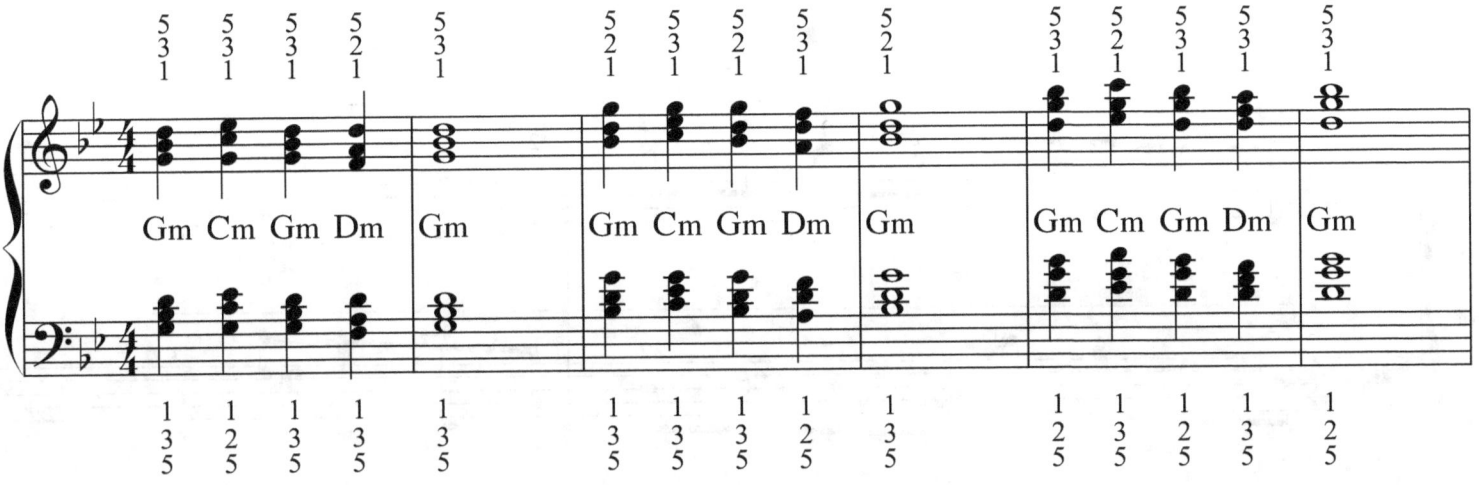

One Octave G Minor Arpeggio

Two Octave G Minor Arpeggios and Inversions

C Minor

Key of C Minor

Five Note Scale

One Octave Scale

Two Octave Scale

Contrary Motion Scale

C minor Chord and Inversions

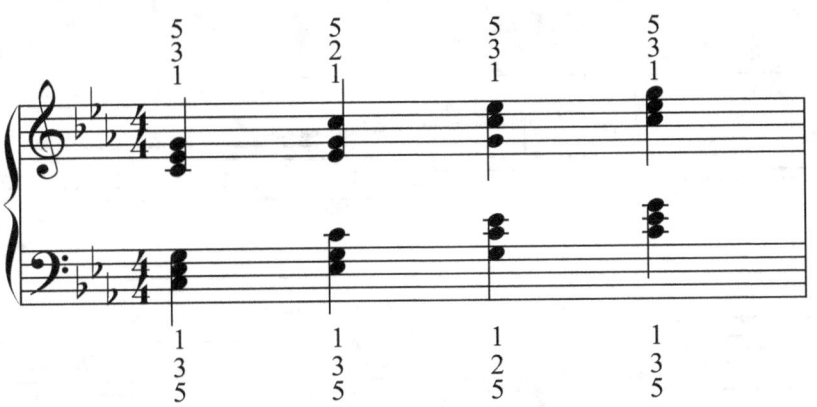

Triads in the Key of C minor

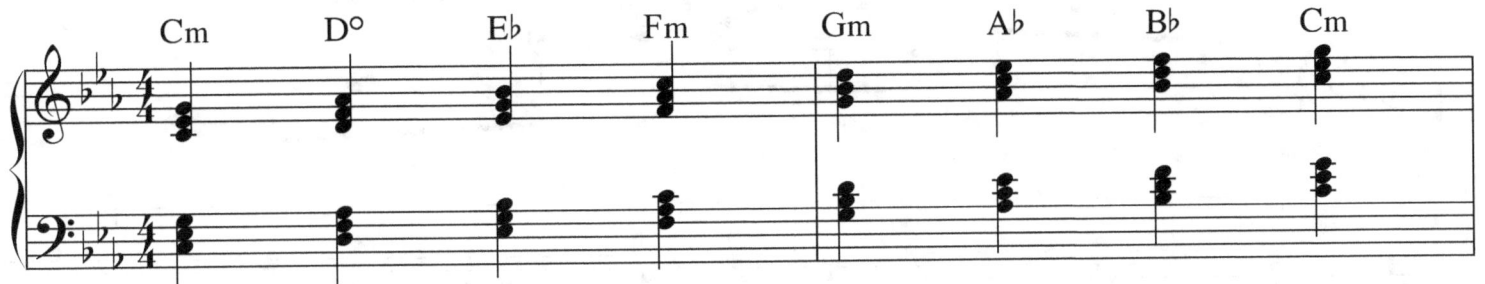

1,4,5 Chord Progression in the Key of C Minor (cadences)

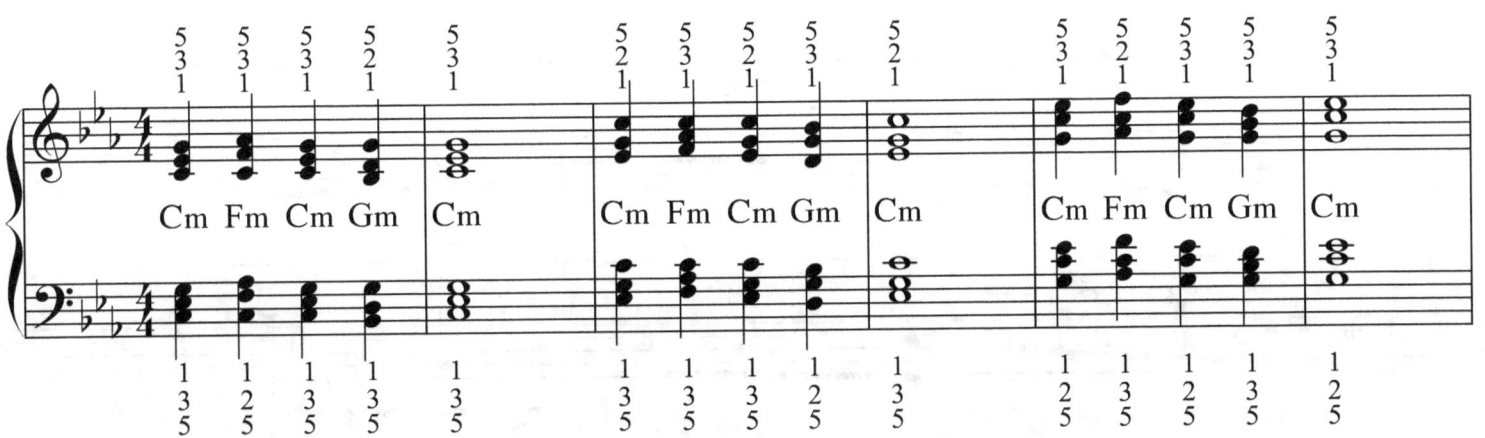

One Octave C Minor Arpeggio

Two Octave C Minor Arpeggios and Inversions

106

F Minor

Key of F Minor

Five Note Scale

One Octave Scale

Two Octave Scale

Contrary Motion Scale

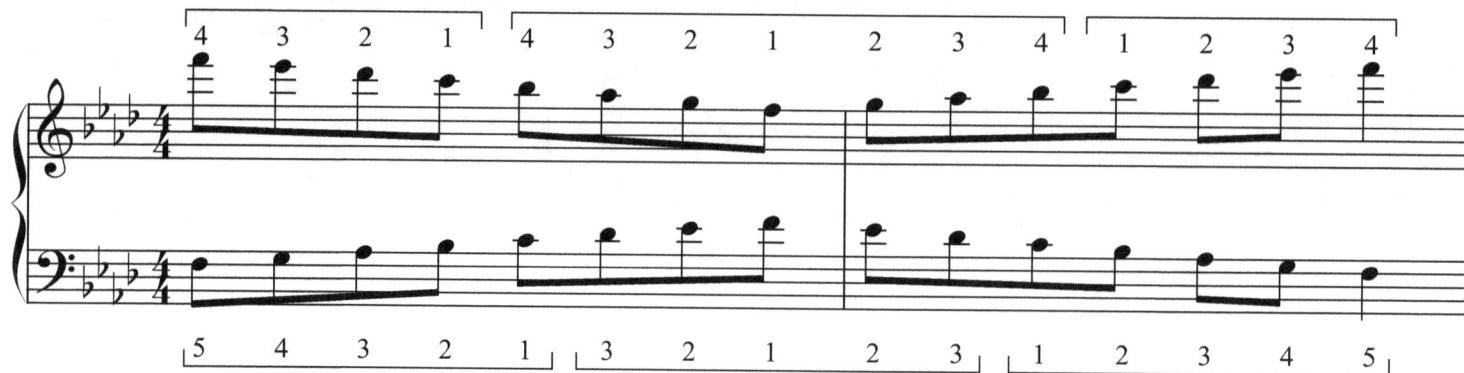

F minor Chord and Inversions

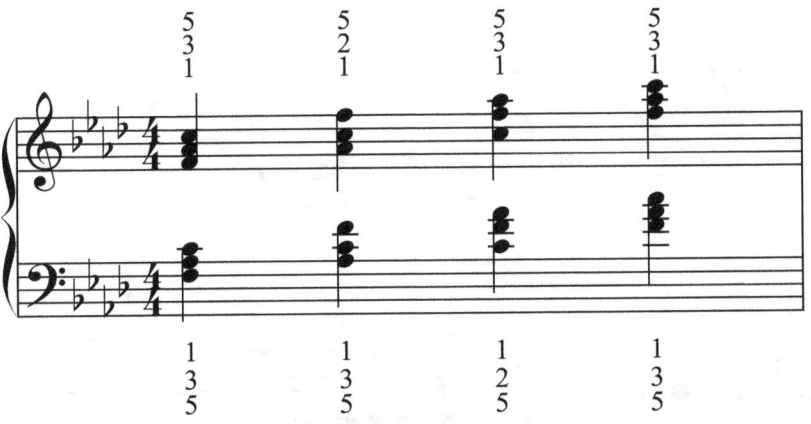

Triads in the Key of F minor

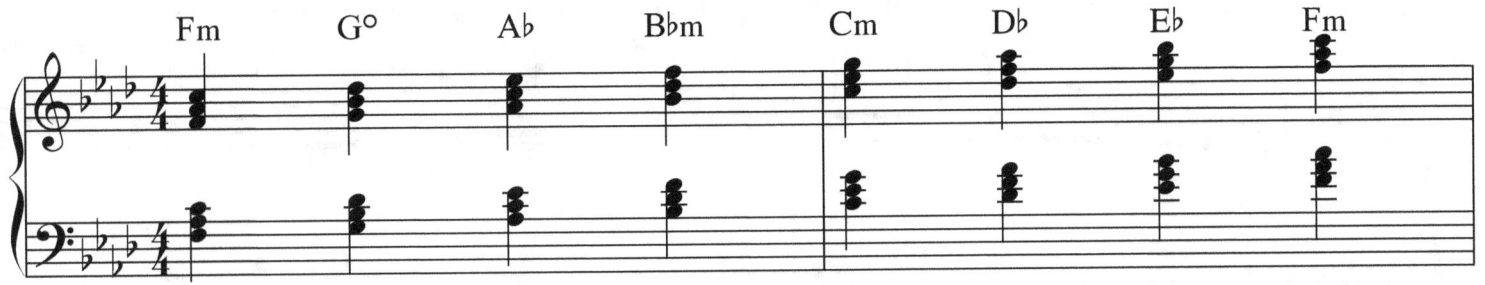

1,4,5 Chord Progression in the Key of F Minor (cadences)

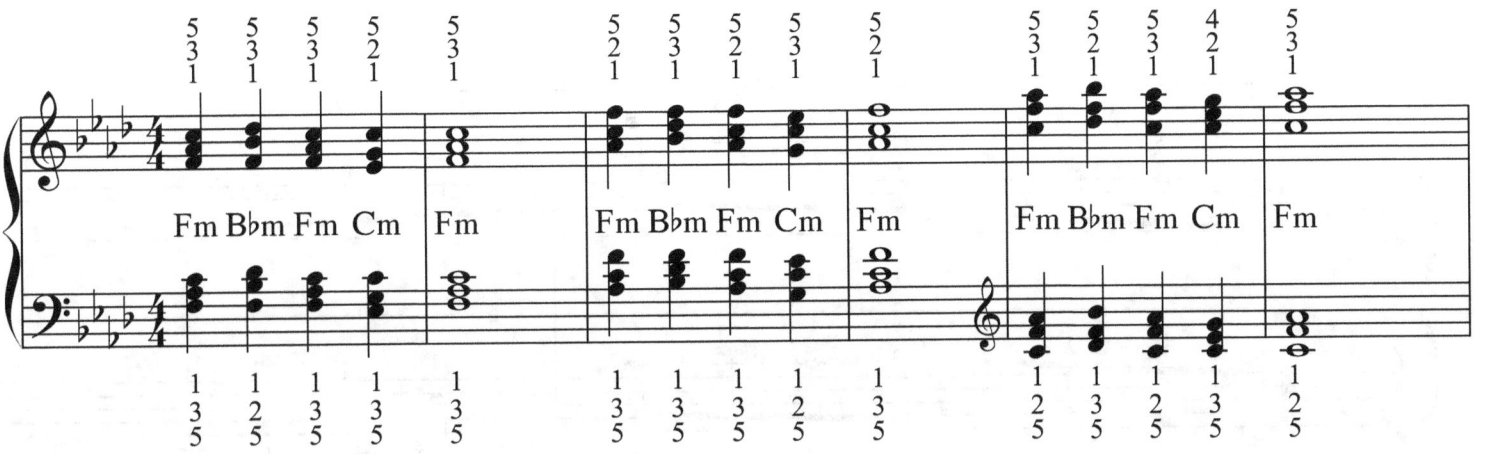

One Octave F Minor Arpeggio

Two Octave F Minor Arpeggios and Inversions

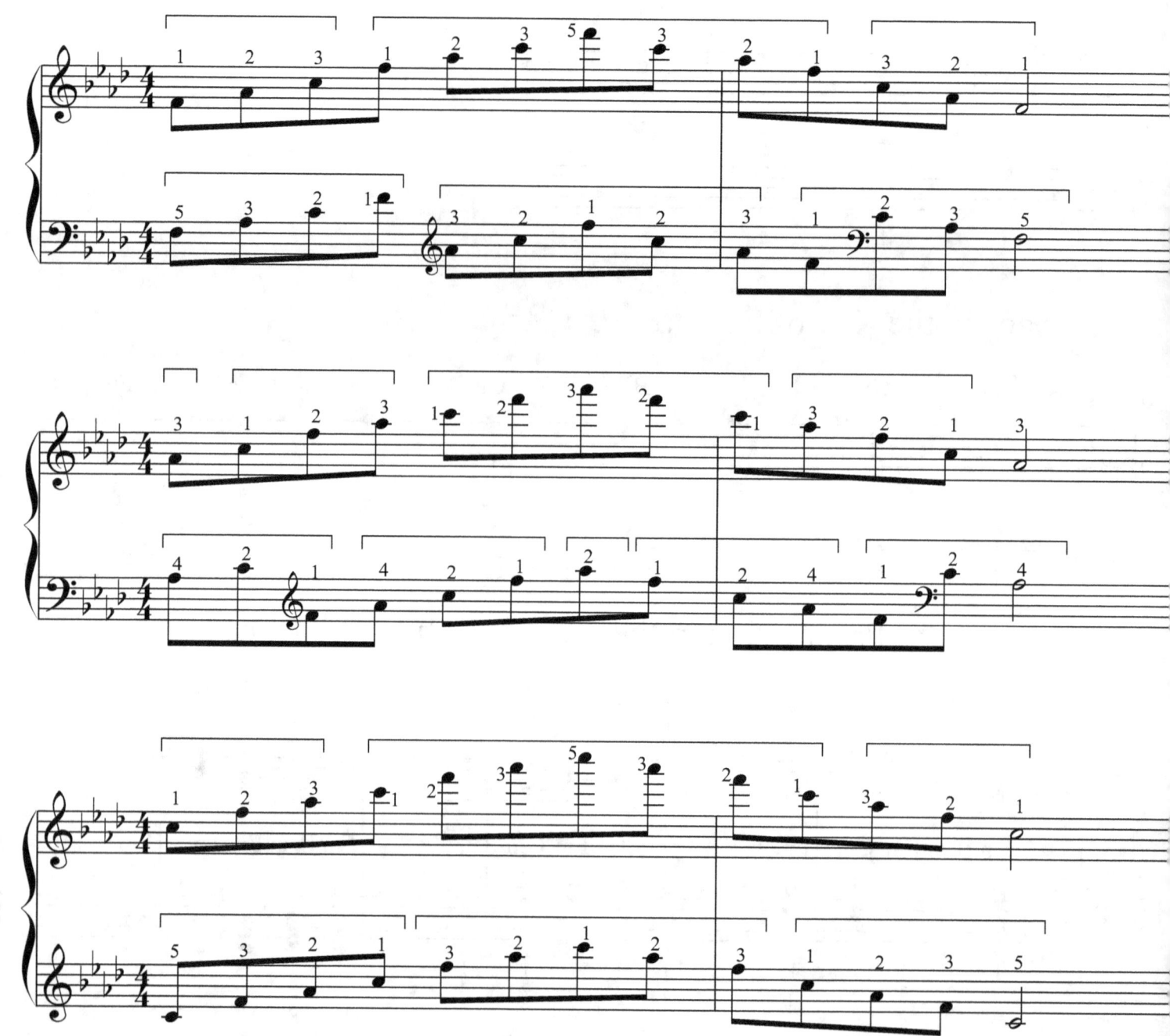

B♭ Minor

Key of B♭ Minor
Enharmonically the same as A#

Five Note Scale

One Octave Scale
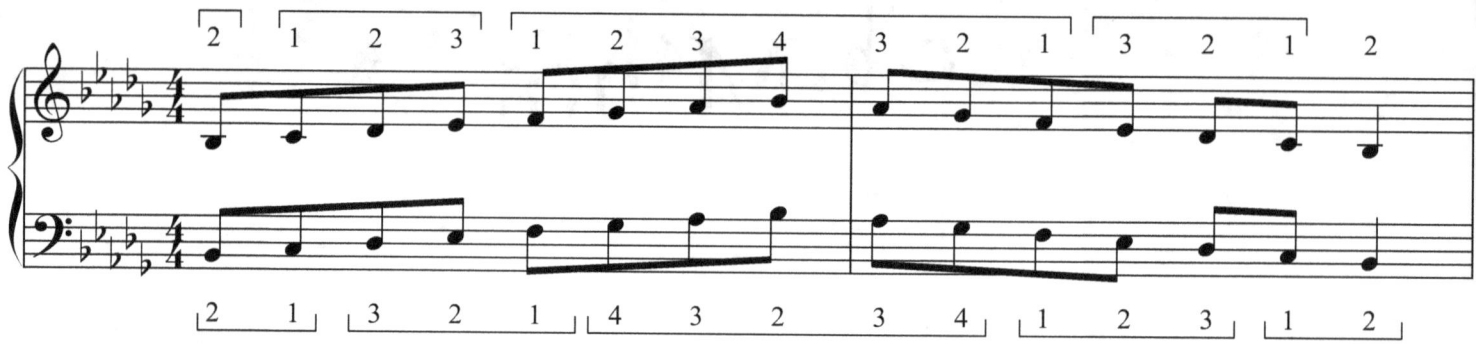

Two Octave Scale

Contrary Motion Scale
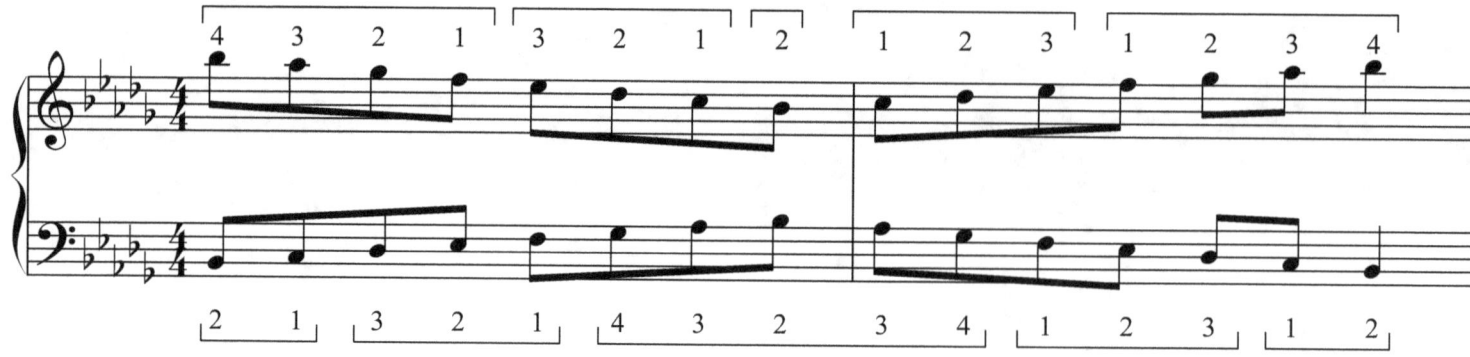

B♭ minor Chord and Inversions

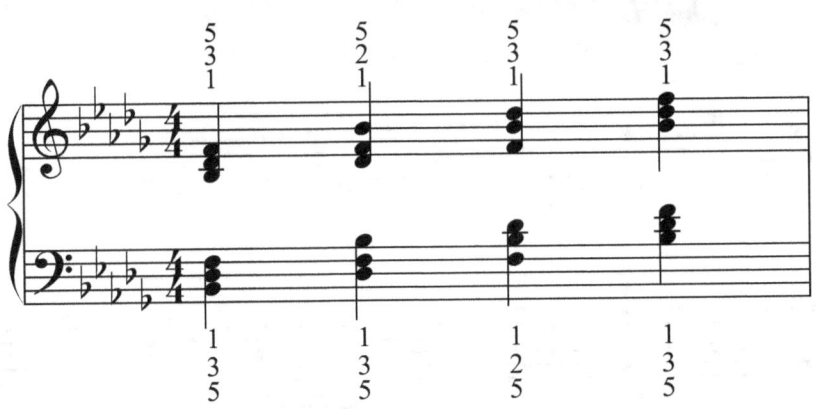

Triads in the Key of B♭ minor

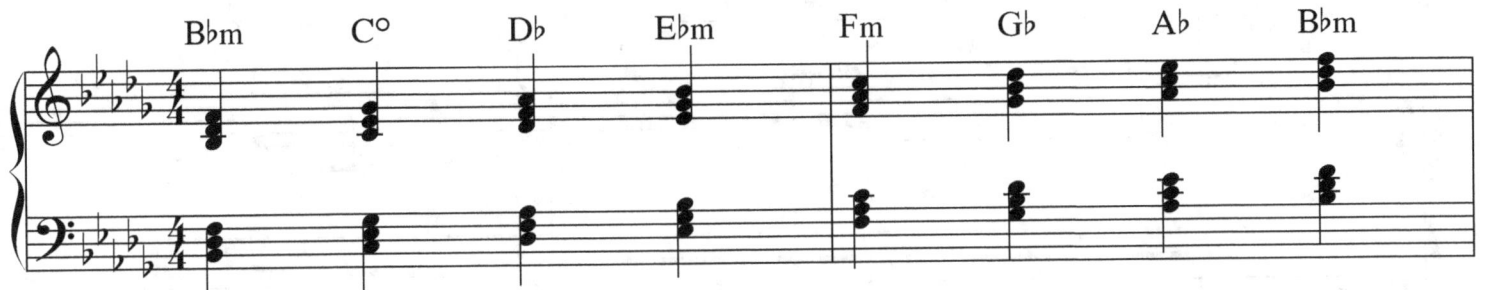

1,4,5 Chord Progression in the Key of B♭ Minor (cadences)

One Octave B♭ Minor Arpeggio

Two Octave B♭ Minor Arpeggios and Inversions

114

E♭ Minor

Key of E♭ Minor
Enharmonically the same as D♯

Five Note Scale

One Octave Scale

Two Octave Scale

Contrary Motion Scale

E♭ minor Chord and Inversions

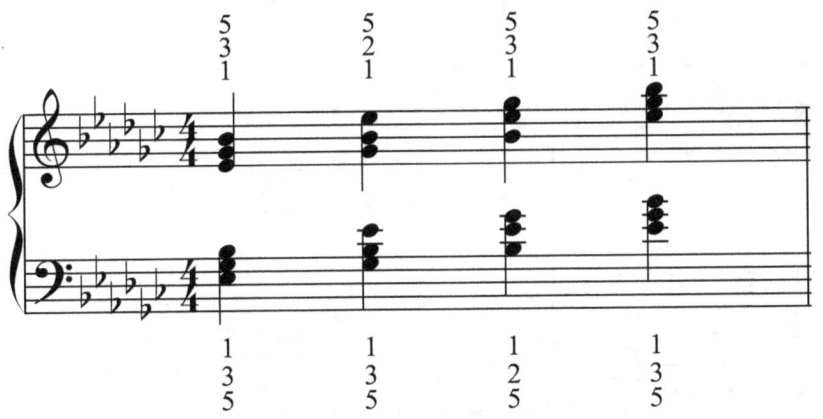

Triads in the Key of E♭ minor

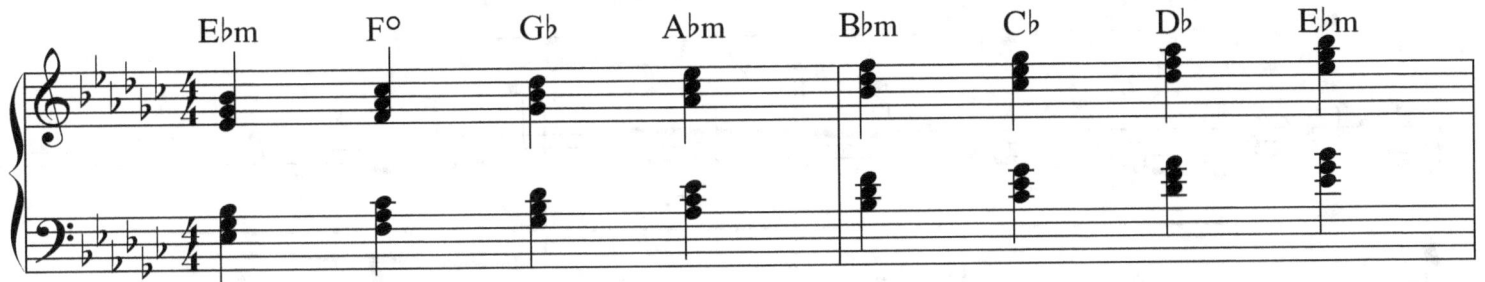

1,4,5 Chord Progression in the Key of E♭ Minor (cadences)

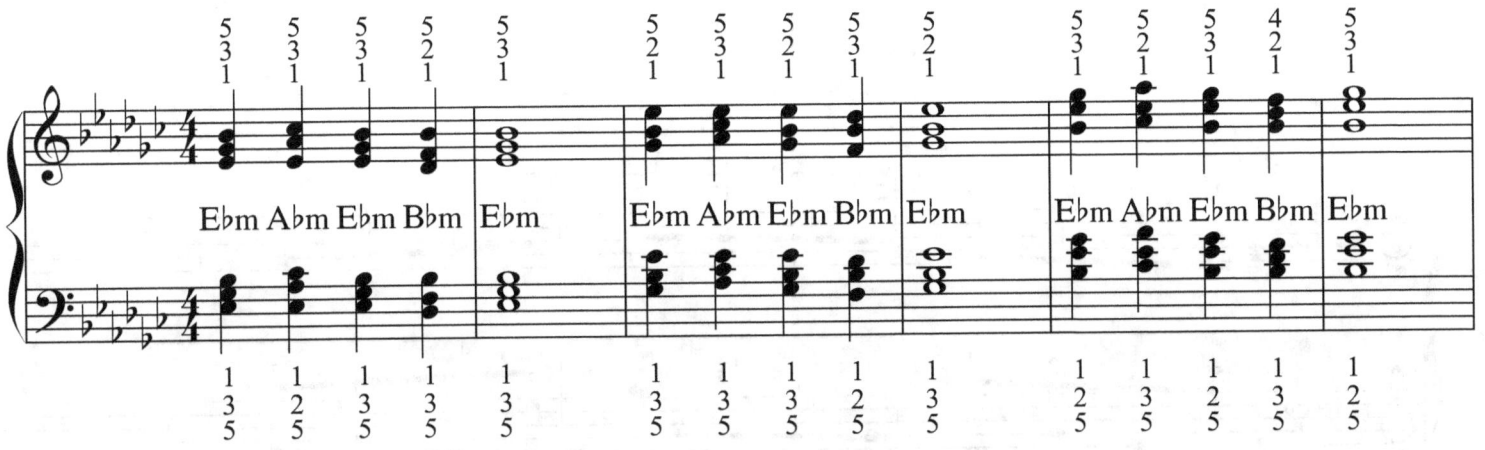

One Octave E♭ Minor Arpeggio

Two Octave E♭ Minor Arpeggios and Inversions

118

Harmonic Minor

A Harmonic Minor.......................... 120
E Harmonic Minor.......................... 121
B Harmonic Minor 122
F♯ Harmonic Minor 123
C♯ Harmonic Minor 124
G♯ Harmonic Minor 125
D Harmonic Minor 126
G Harmonic Minor 127
C Harmonic Minor 128
F Harmonic Minor........................... 129
B♭ Harmonic Minor 130
E♭ Harmonic Minor 131

A Harmonic Minor

A Harmonic Minor Scale

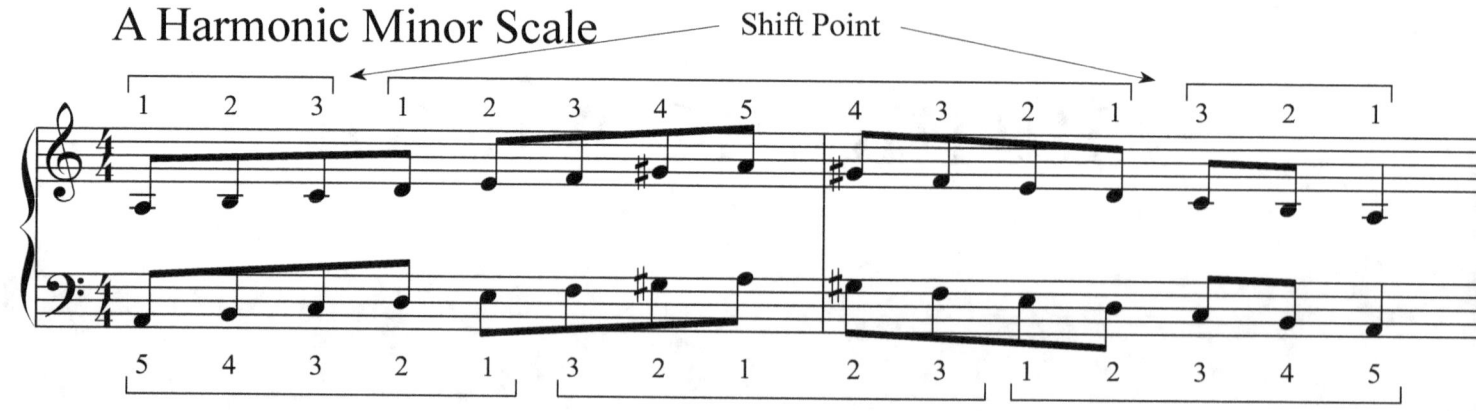

A Harmonic Minor Chords

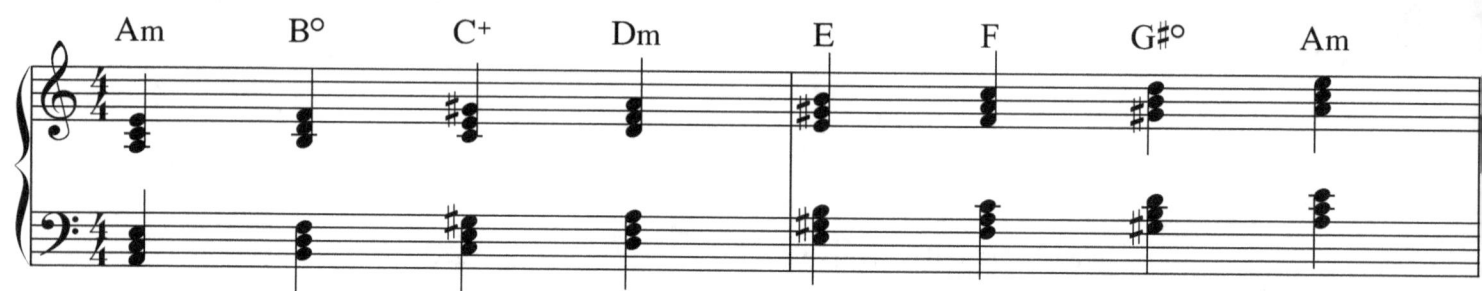

1,4,5 Chord Progression A Harmonic Minor (Cadences)

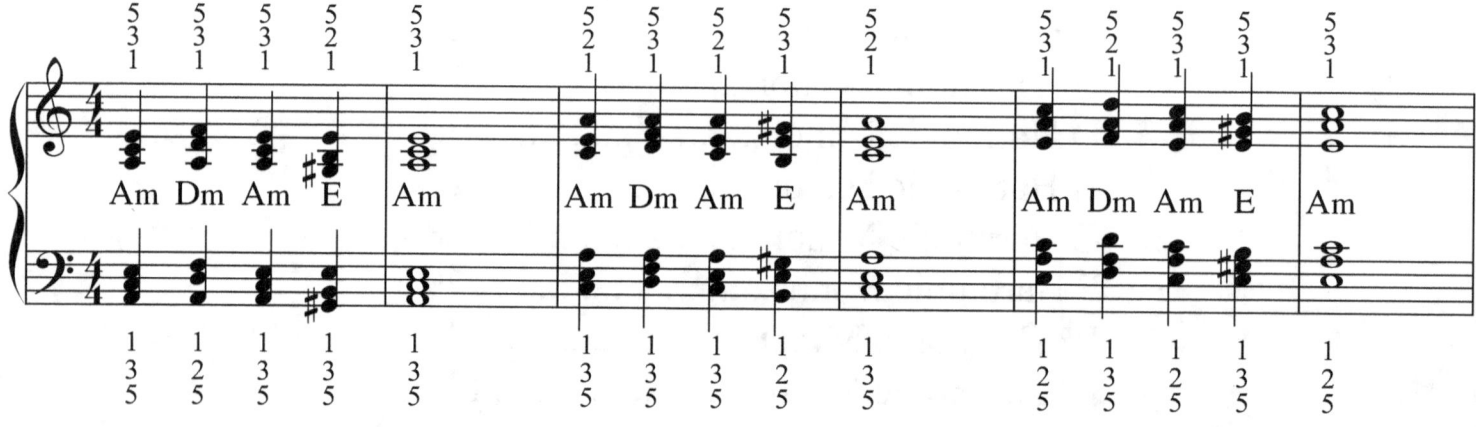

E Harmonic Minor

E Harmonic Minor Scale

E Harmonic Minor Chords

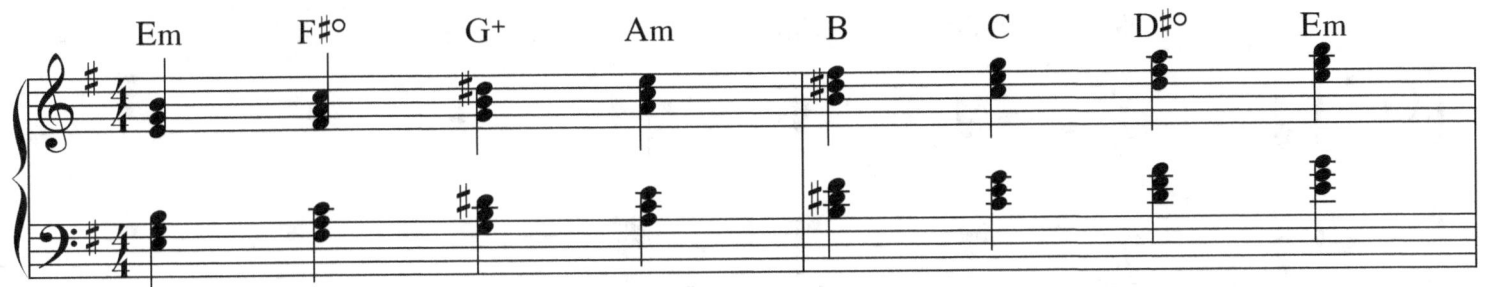

1,4,5 Chord Progression E Harmonic Minor (Cadences)

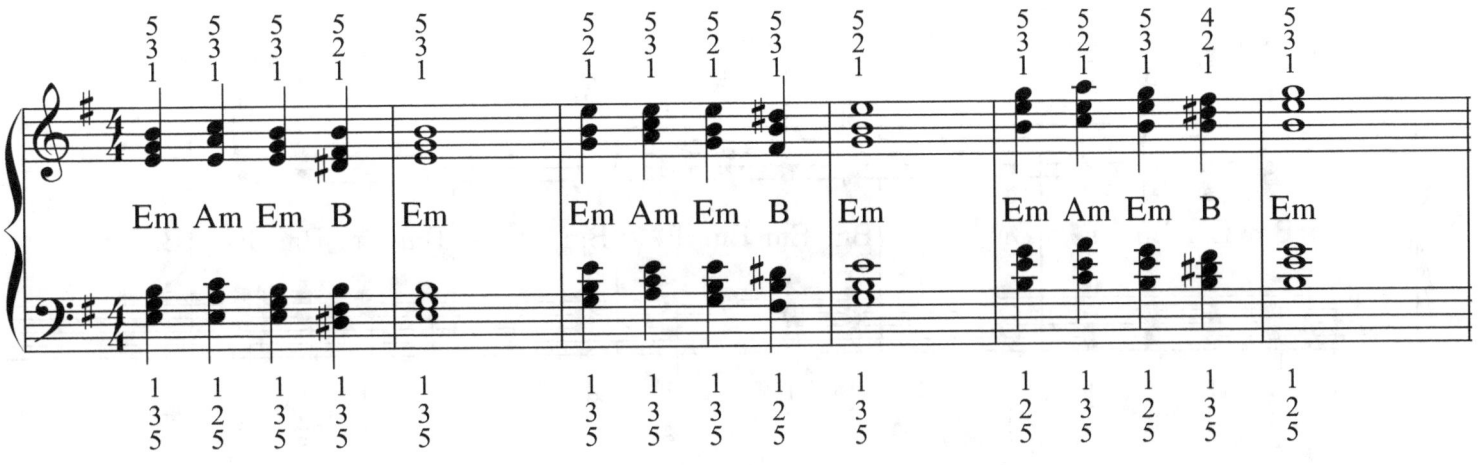

B Harmonic Minor

B Harmonic Minor Scale

B Harmonic Minor Chords

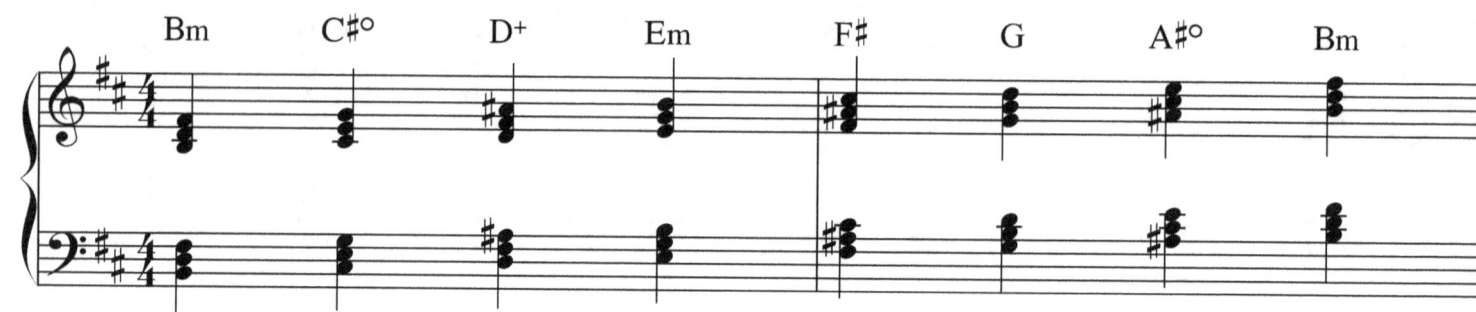

1,4,5 Chord Progression B Harmonic Minor (Cadences)

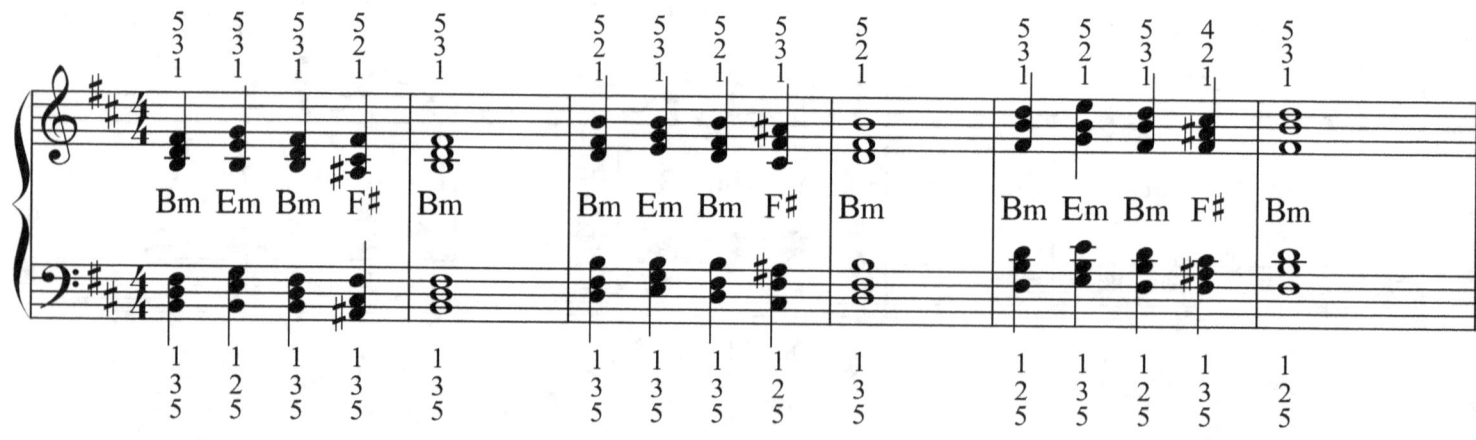

F# Harmonic Minor
Enharmonically the same as G♭

F# Harmonic Minor Scale

F# Harmonic Minor Chords

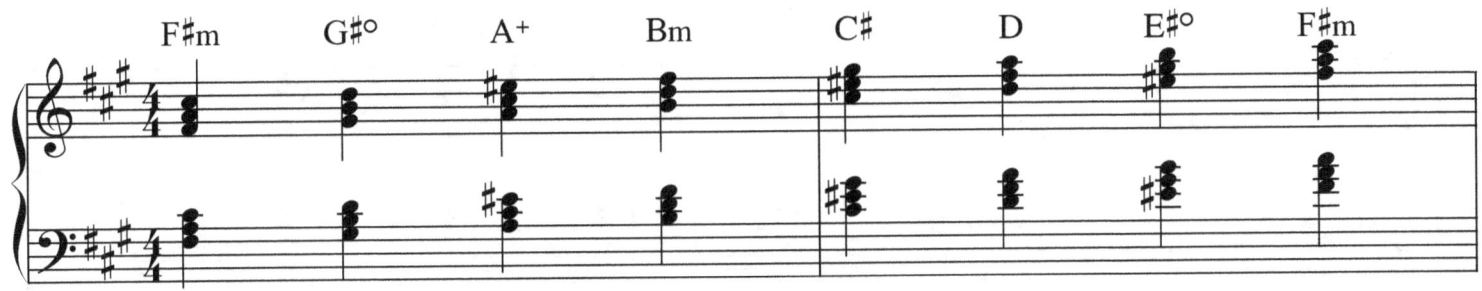

1,4,5 Chord Progression F# Harmonic Minor (Cadences)

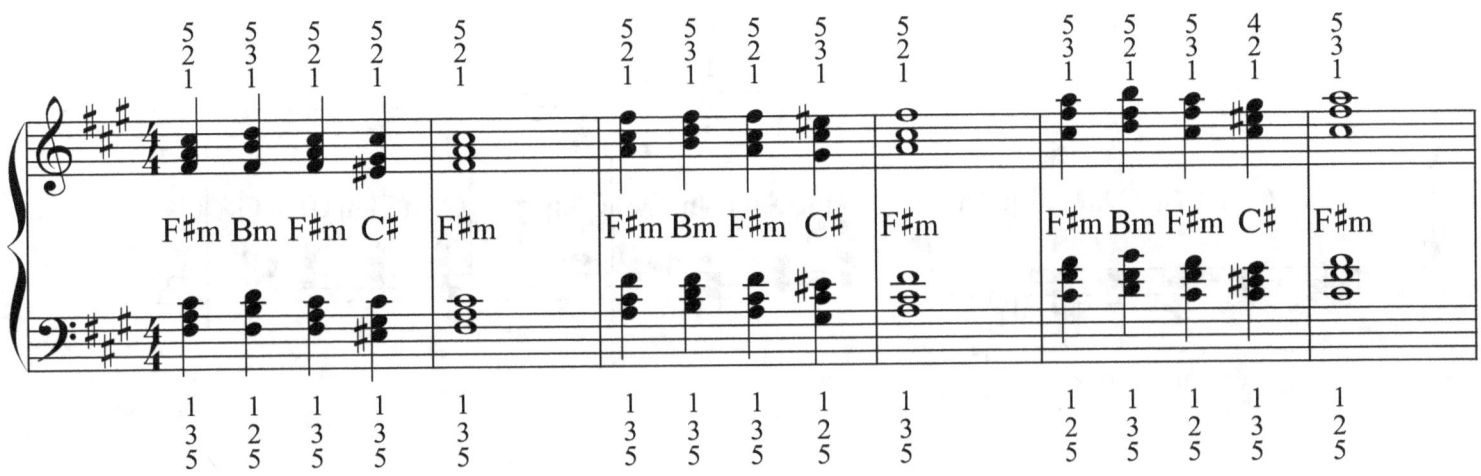

C# Harmonic Minor

Enharmonically the same as D♭

C# Harmonic Minor Scale

C# Harmonic Minor Chords

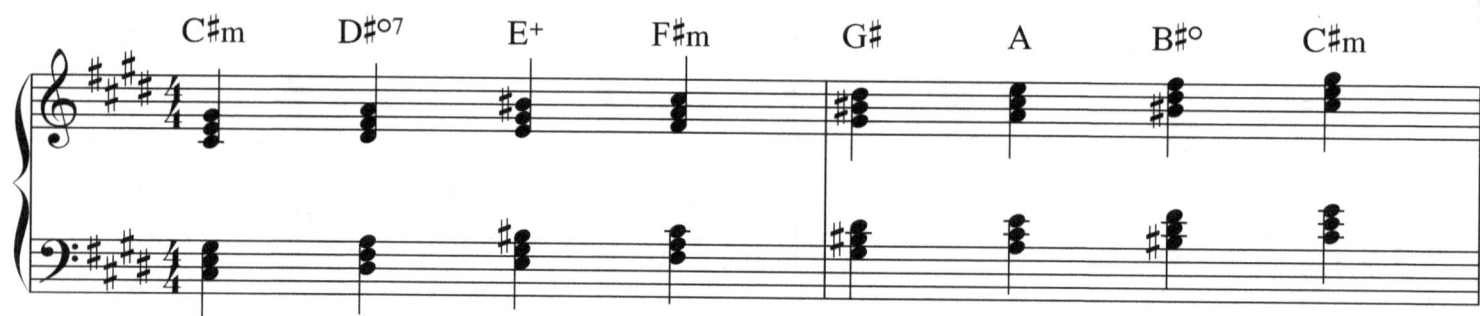

1,4,5 Chord Progression C# Harmonic Minor (Cadences)

G♯ Harmonic Minor

Enharmonically the same as A♭

G♯ Harmonic Minor Scale

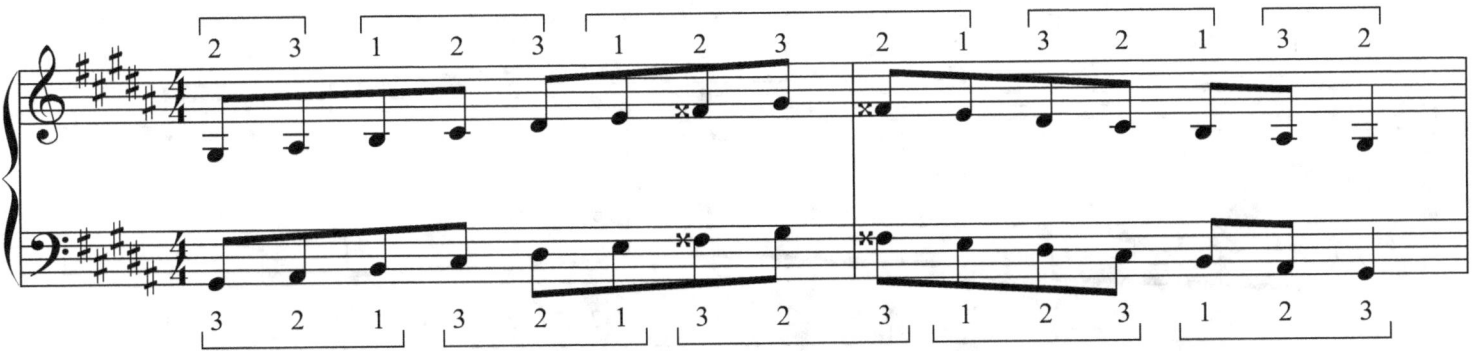

G♯ Harmonic Minor Chords

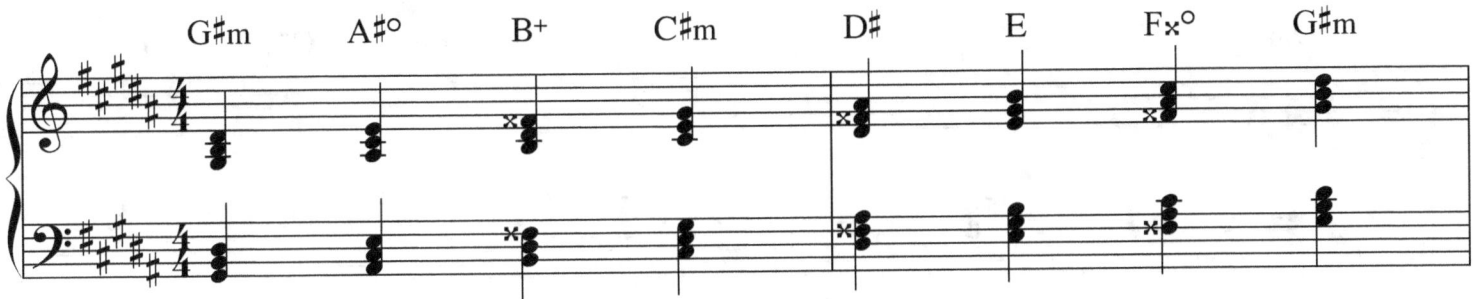

1,4,5 Chord Progression G♯ Harmonic Minor (Cadences)

D Harmonic Minor

D Harmonic Minor Scale

D Harmonic Minor Chords

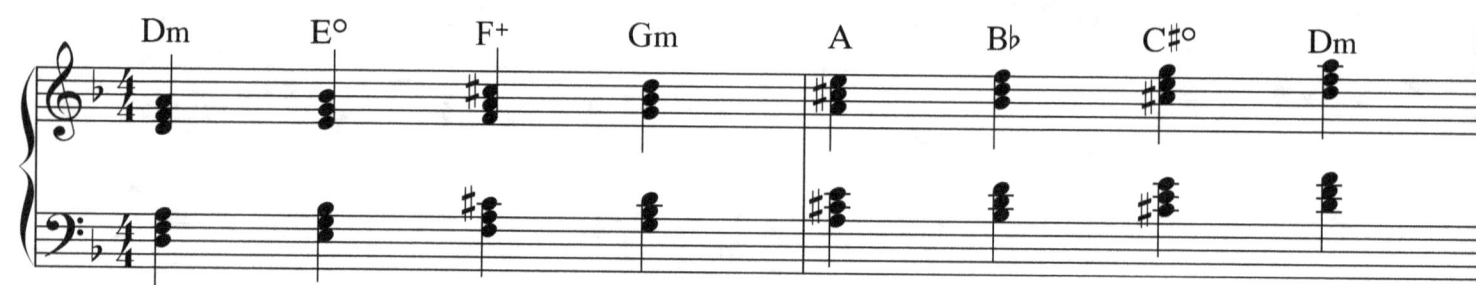

1,4,5 Chord Progression D Harmonic Minor (Cadences)

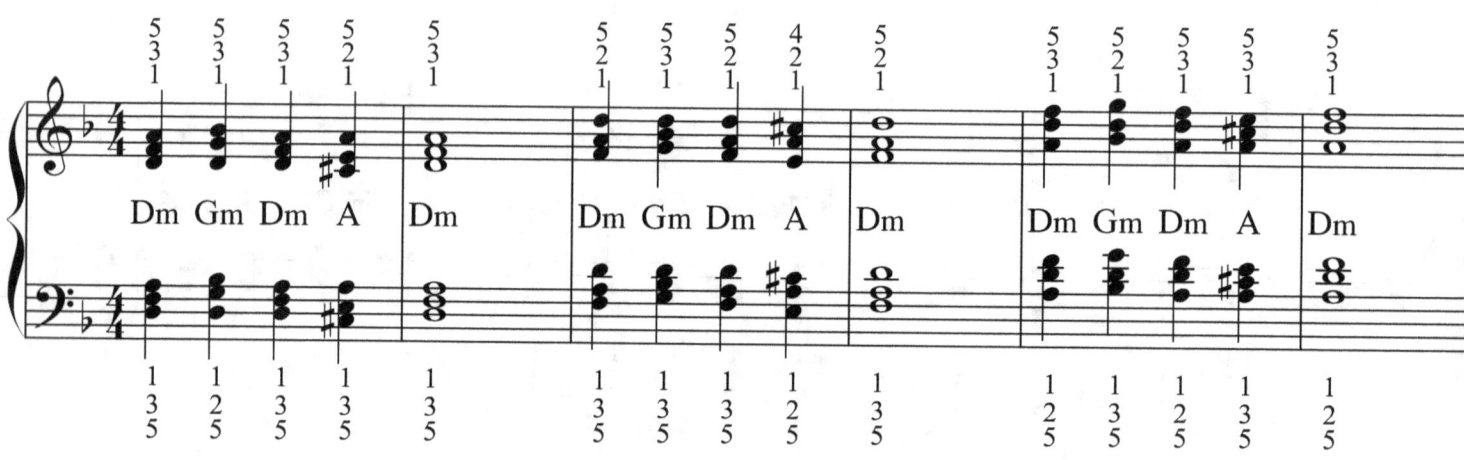

G Harmonic Minor

G Harmonic Minor Scale

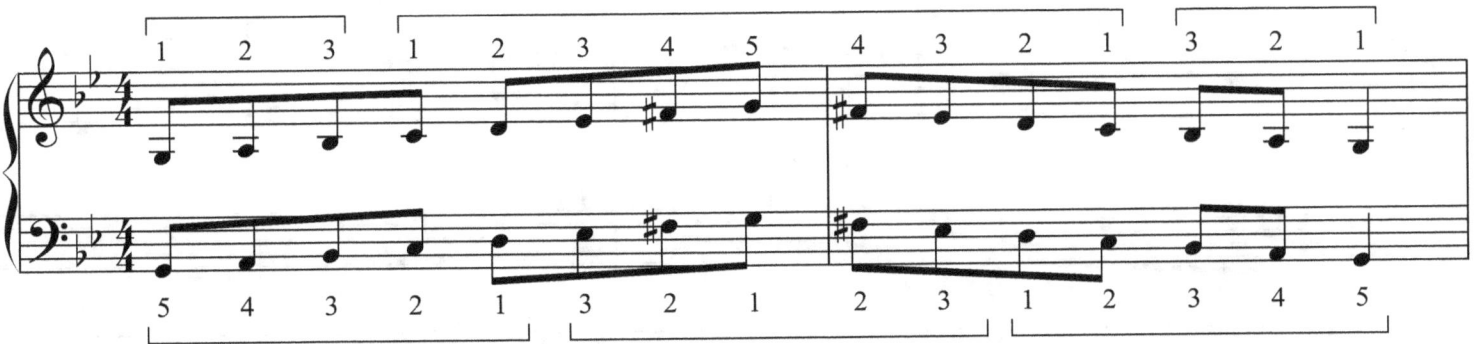

G Harmonic Minor Chords

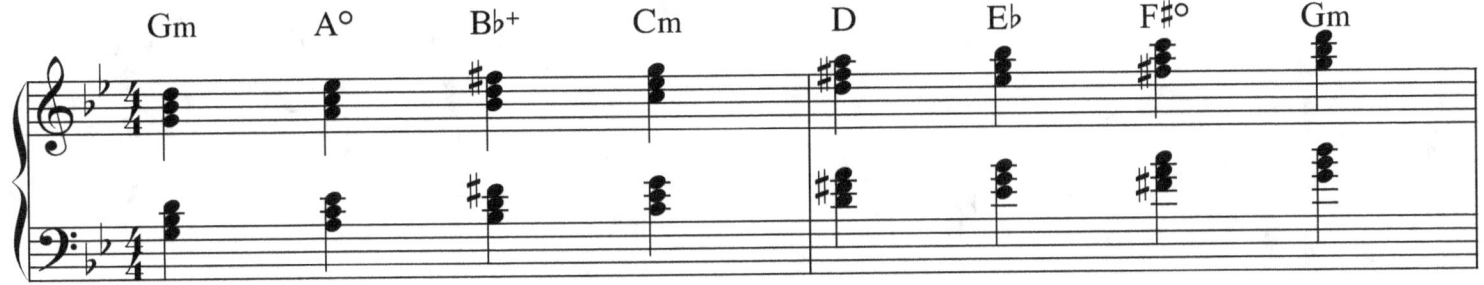

1,4,5 Chord Progression G Harmonic Minor (Cadences)

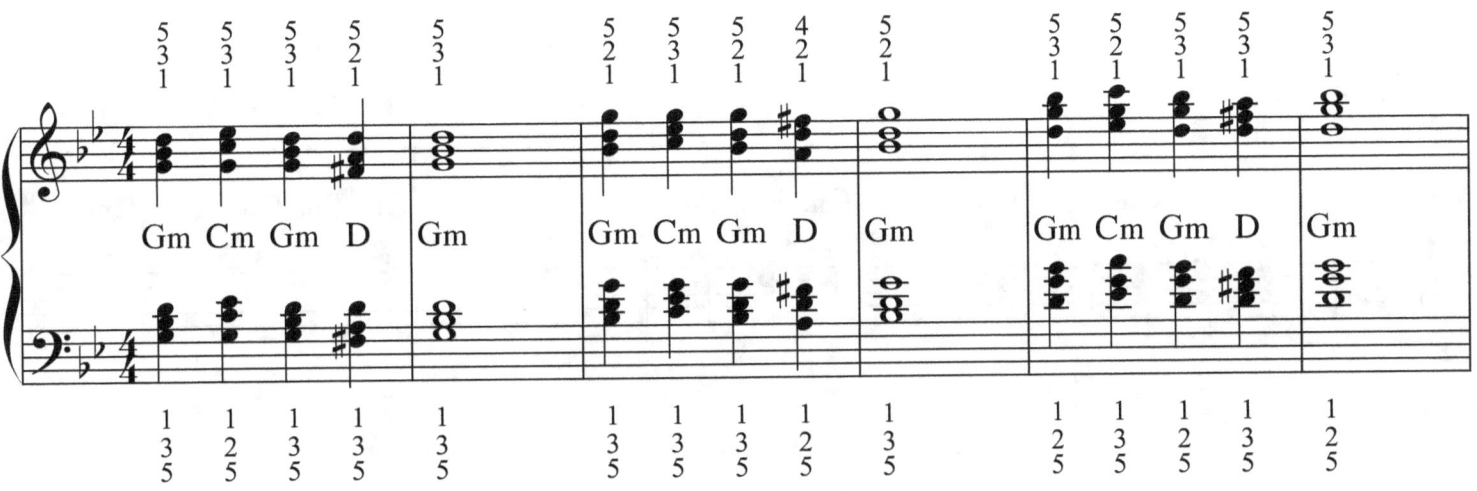

C Harmonic Minor

C Harmonic Minor Scale

C Harmonic Minor Chords

1,4,5 Chord Progression C Harmonic Minor (Cadences)

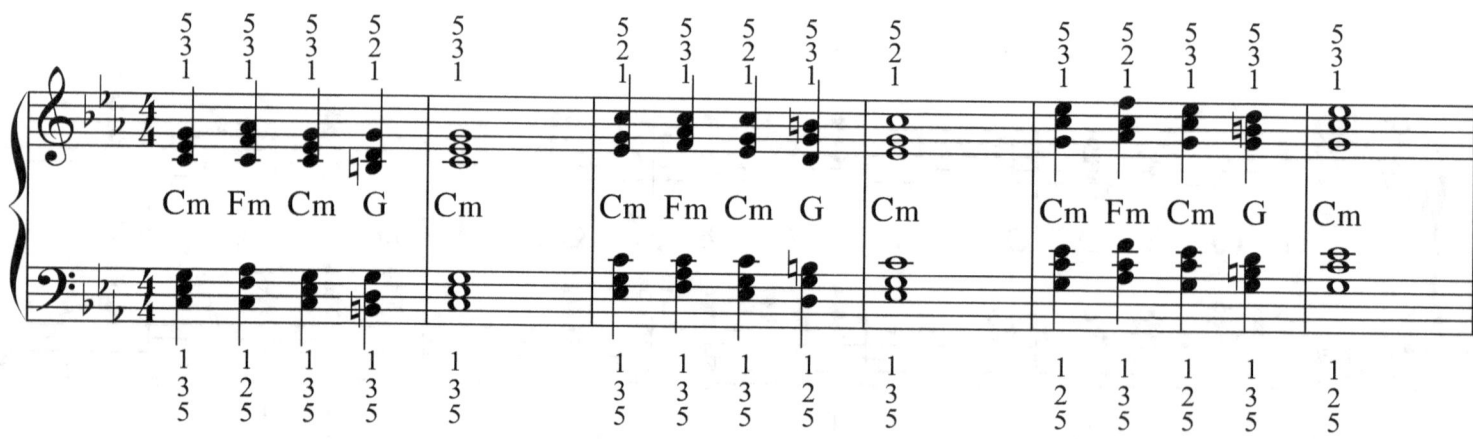

F Harmonic Minor

F Harmonic Minor Scale

F Harmonic Minor Chords

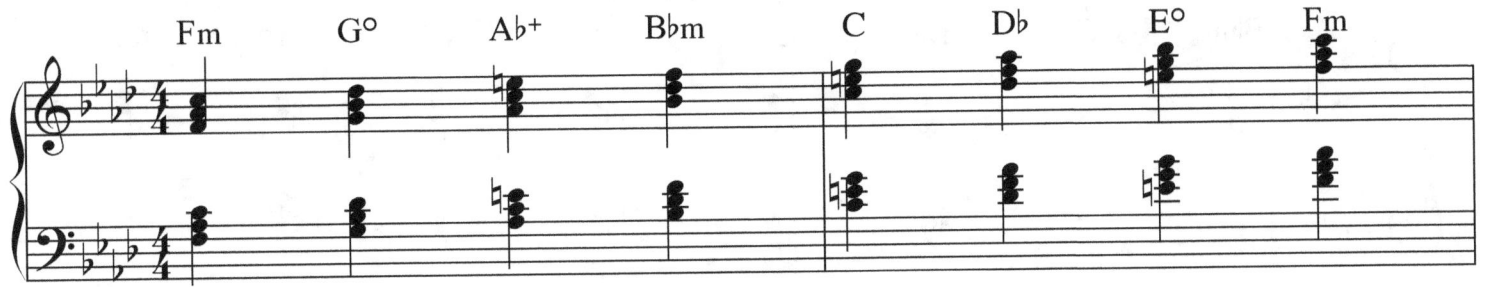

1,4,5 Chord Progression F Harmonic Minor (Cadences)

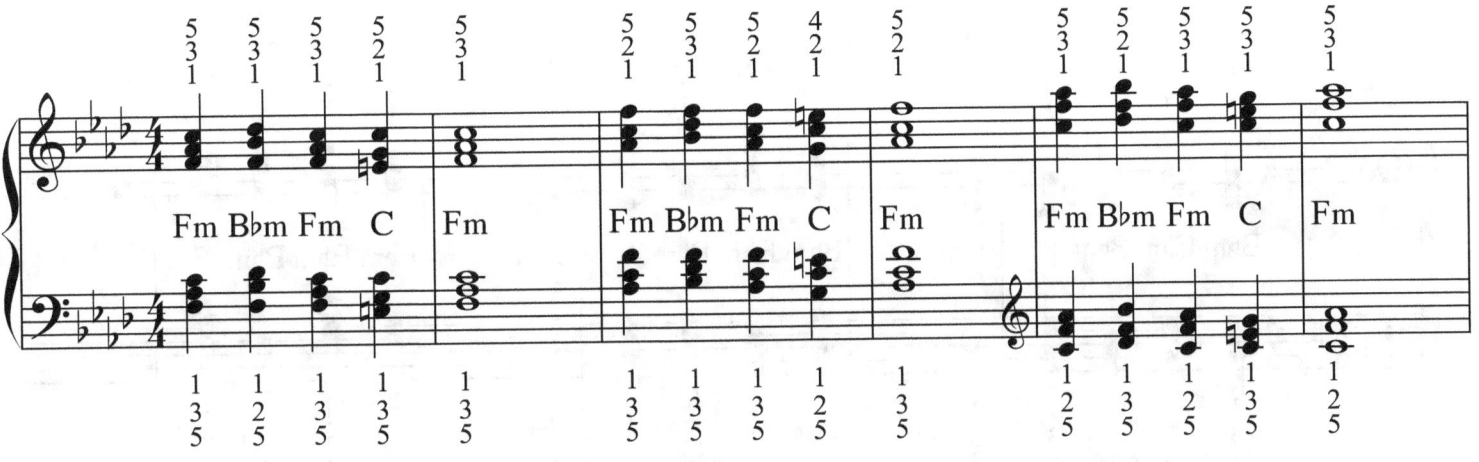

B♭ Harmonic Minor

Enharmonically the same as A♯

B♭ Harmonic Minor Scale

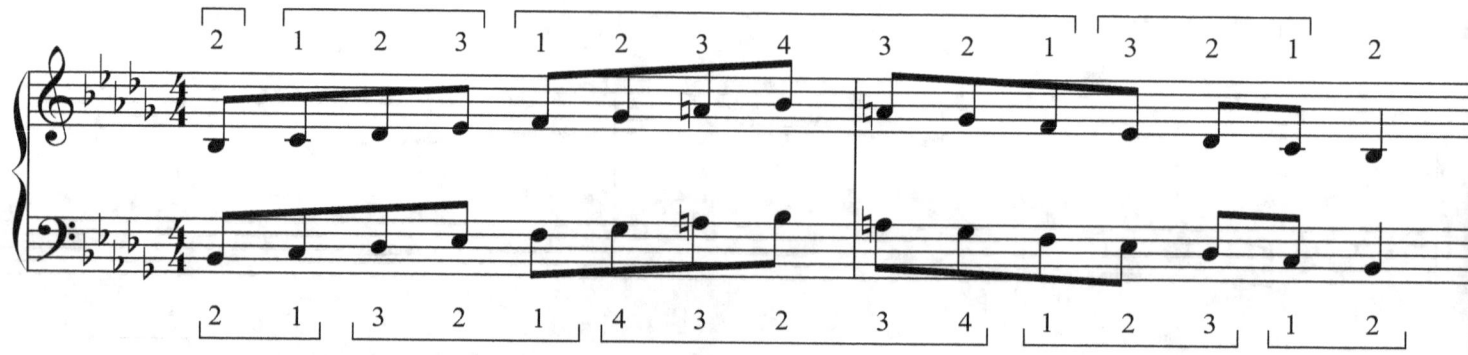

B♭ Harmonic Minor Chords

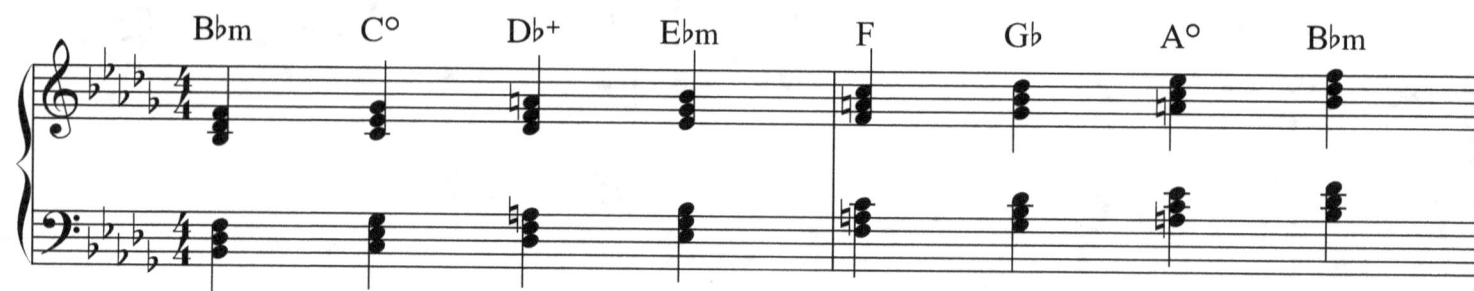

1,4,5 Chord Progression B♭ Harmonic Minor (Cadences)

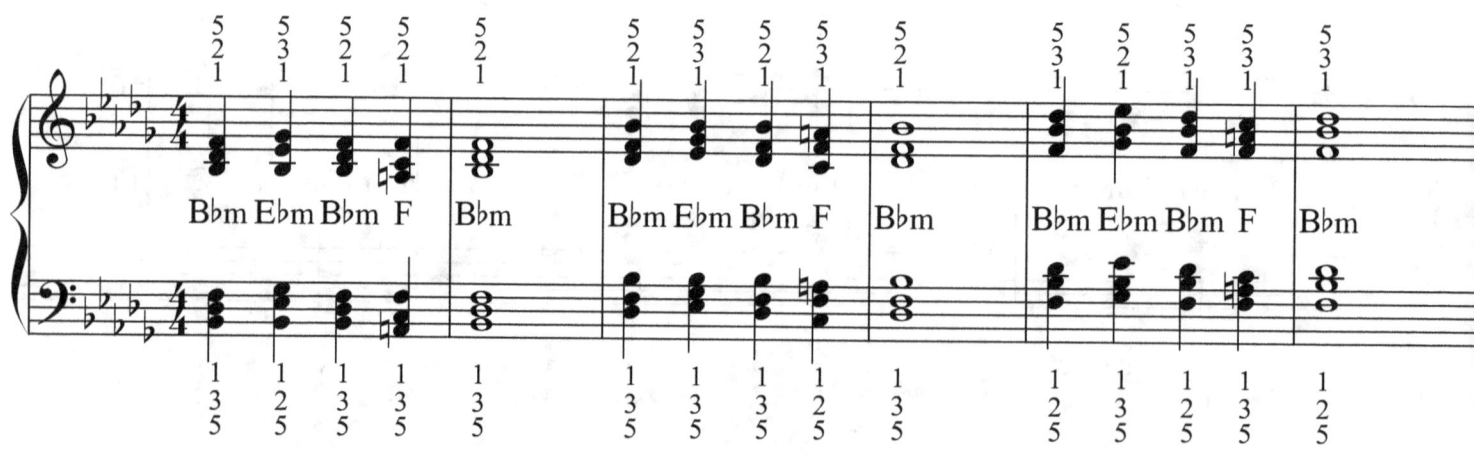

E♭ Harmonic Minor
Enharmonically the same as D♯

E♭ Harmonic Minor Scale

E♭ Harmonic Minor Chords

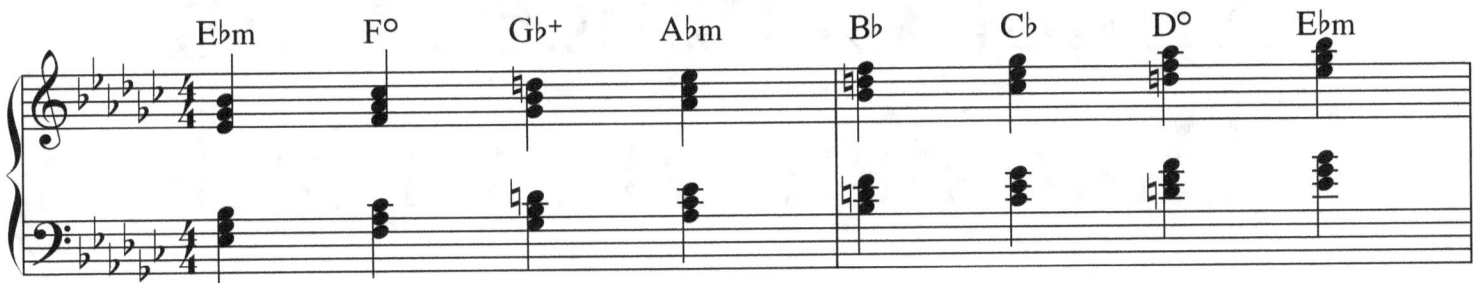

1,4,5 Chord Progression E♭ Harmonic Minor (Cadences)

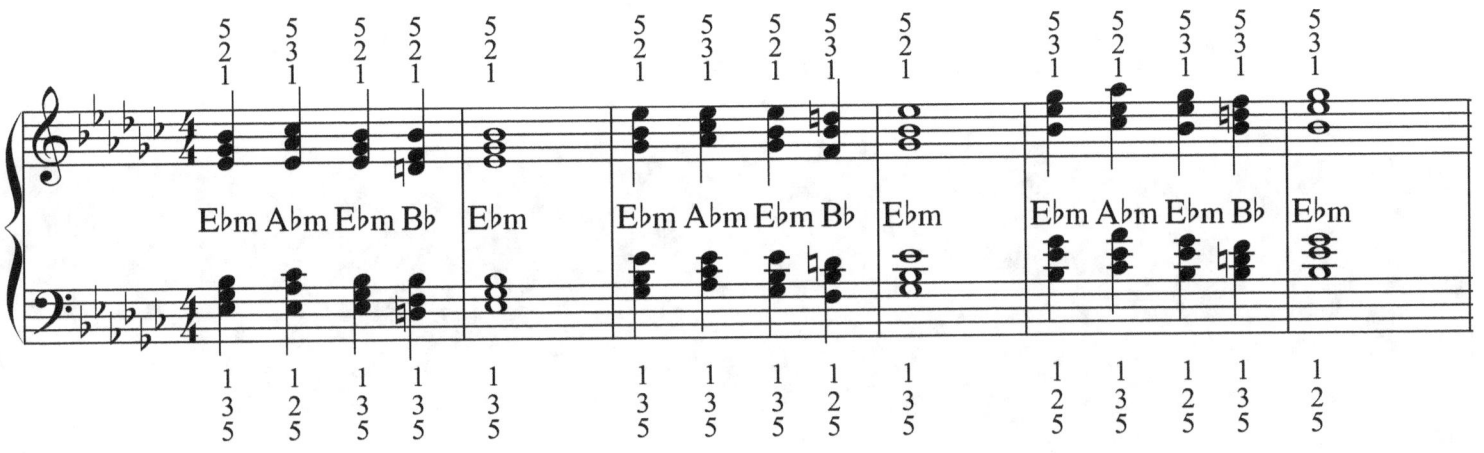

Minor Cadences with Dominant 7th Chord

Note - The Minor Cadences are presented in order of the number of sharps and flats in the key (Am no sharps, Em 1 sharp, Dm 2 sharps, etc.).

Melodic Minor Scales

Note - The Melodic Minor Scales are presented in order of the number of sharps and flats in the key (A Melodic Minor no sharps, E Melodic Minor 1 sharp, B Melodic Minor 2 sharps, etc.).

A Melodic Minor

E Melodic Minor

B Melodic Minor

F# Melodic Minor

C# Melodic Minor

G# Melodic Minor

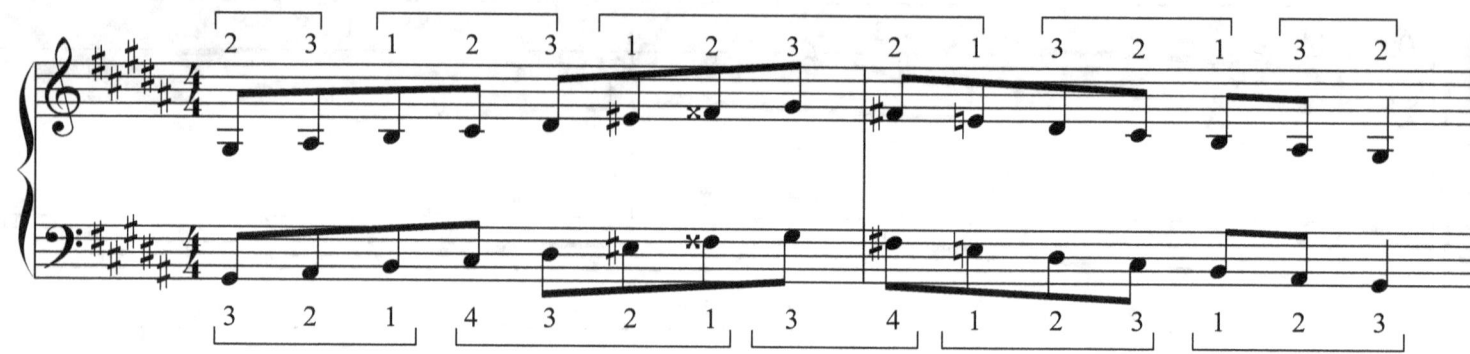

D Melodic Minor

G Melodic Minor

C Melodic Minor

F Melodic Minor

B♭ Melodic Minor

E♭ Melodic Minor

Chromatic Scales

Chromatic Scale Up and Down a Fifth

One Octave Chromatic Scale

Contrary Motion Chromatic Scale

Major Pentatonic Scales

Note - The Major Pentatonic Scales are presented in order of the number of sharps and flats in the key (C no sharps, G 1 sharp, D 2 sharps, etc.).

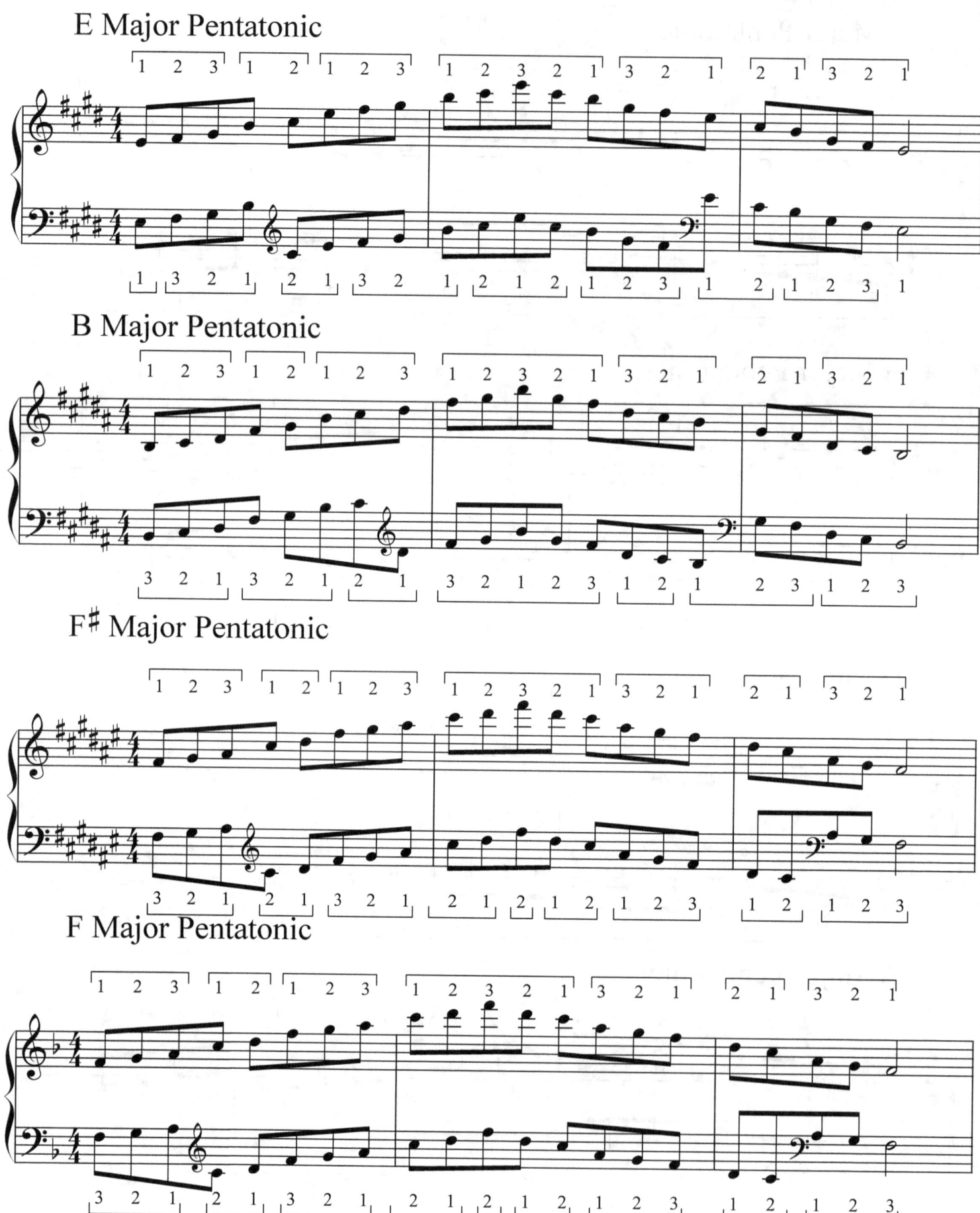

B♭ Major Pentatonic

E♭ Major Pentatonic

A♭ Major Pentatonic

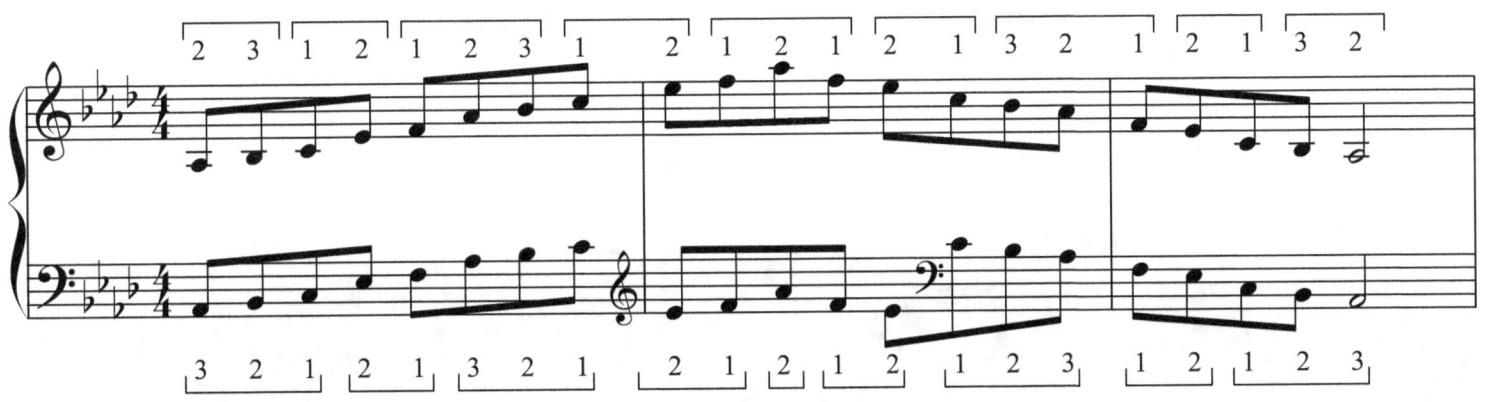

D♭ Major Pentatonic

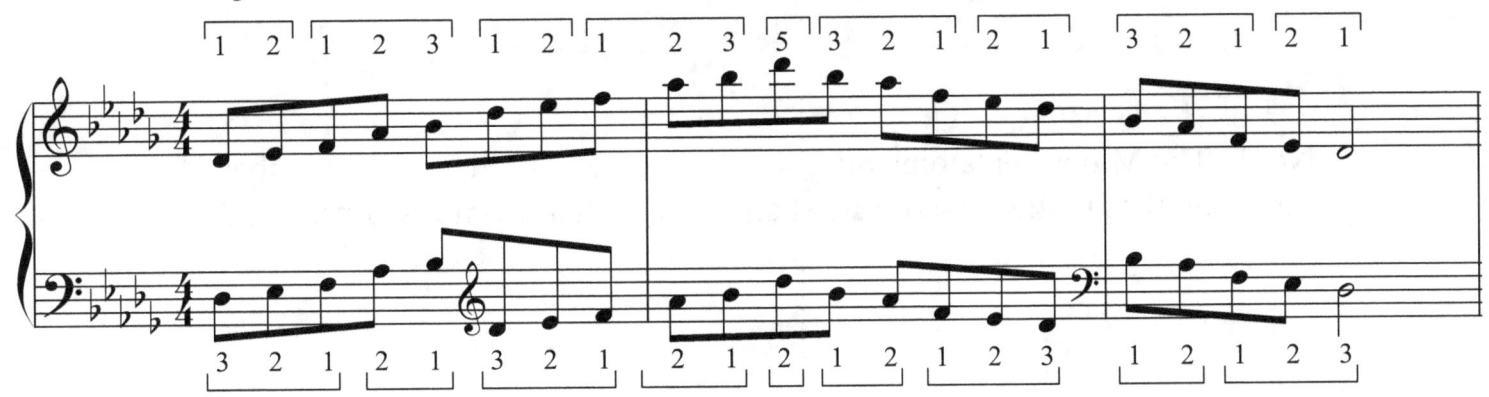

Minor Pentatonic Scales

Note - The Minor Pentatonic Scales are presented in order of the number of sharps and flats in the key (Am no sharps, Em 1 sharp, Bm 2 sharps, etc.).

A Minor Pentatonic

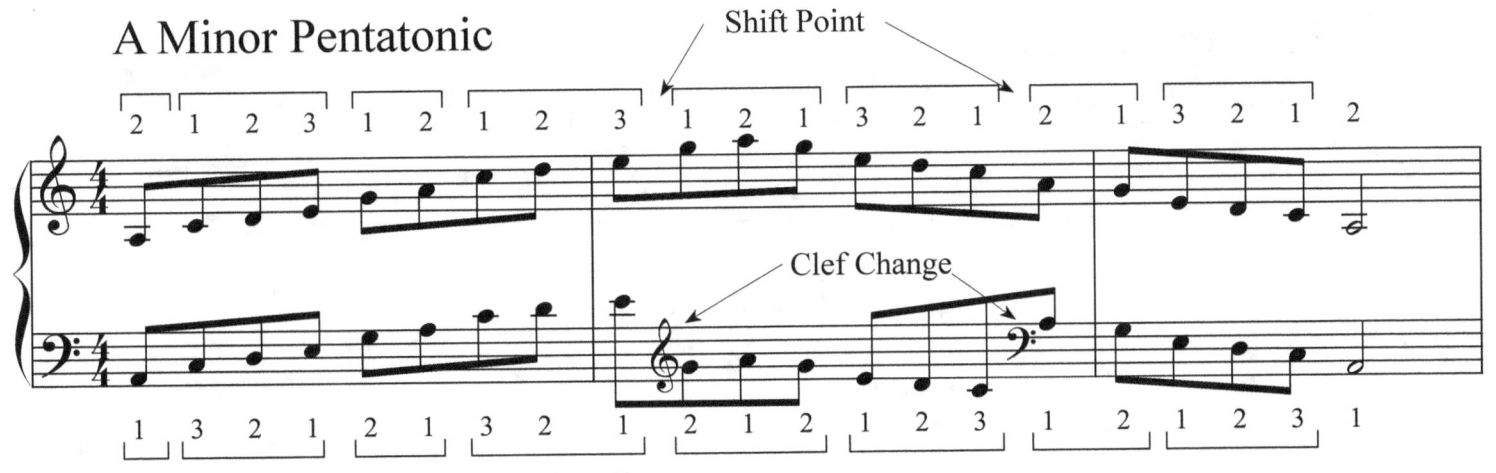

E Minor Pentatonic

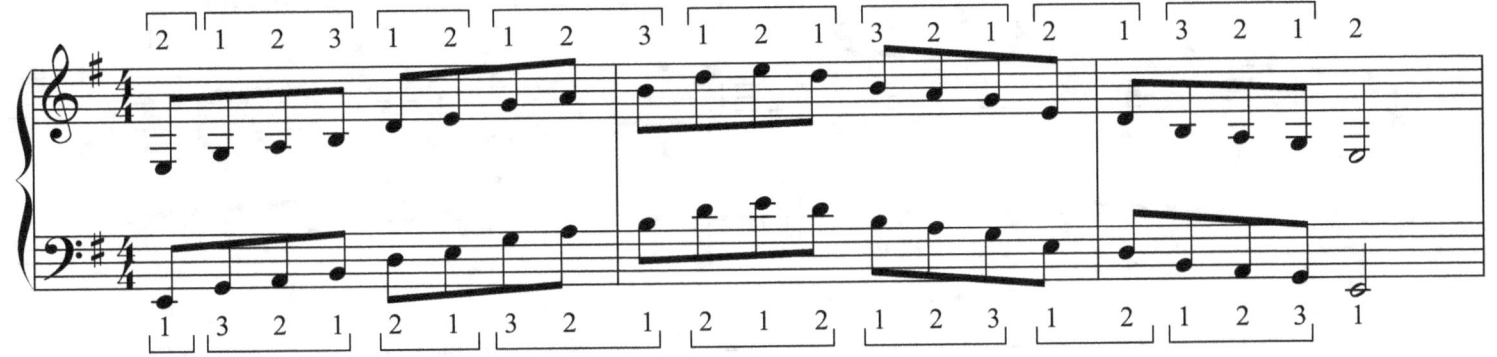

B Minor Pentatonic

F# Minor Pentatonic

C# Minor Pentatonic

G# Minor Pentatonic

D Minor Pentatonic

G Minor Pentatonic

C Minor Pentatonic

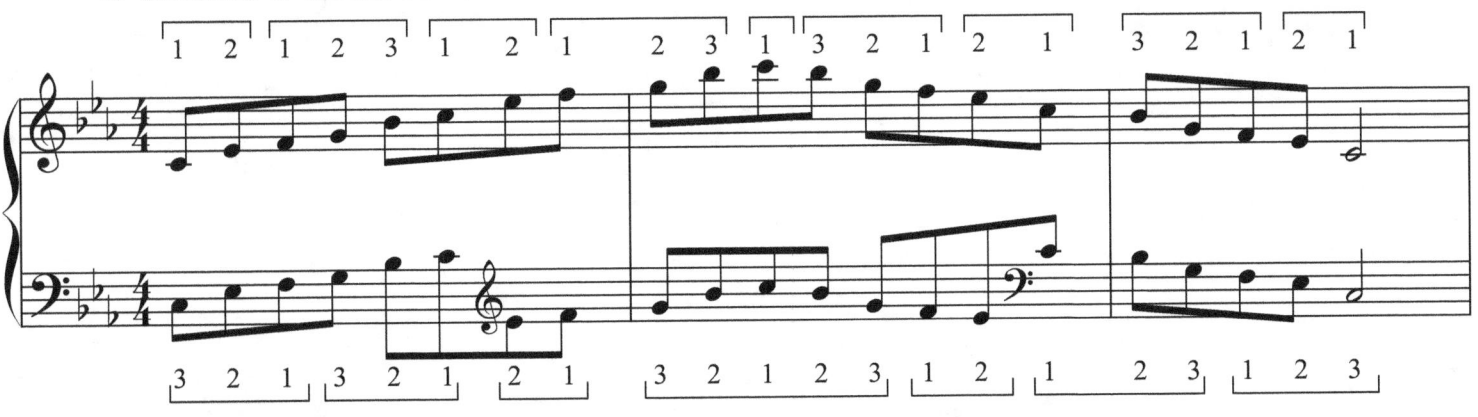

F Minor Pentatonic

B♭ Minor Pentatonic

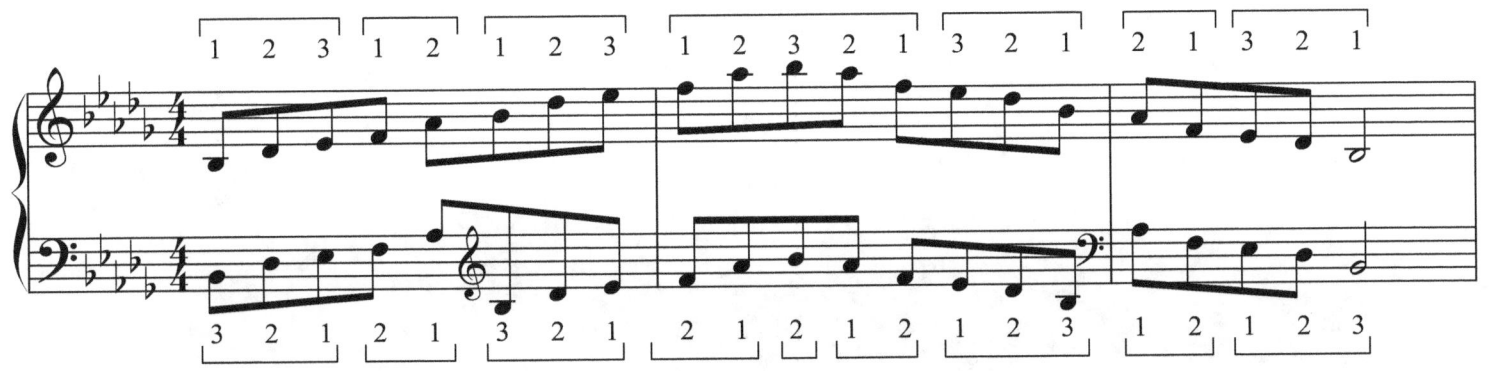

E♭ Minor Pentatonic

Enharmonic Keys

F# Major

Enharmonically the same as G♭ - refer to page 63

Two Octave Scale

Two Octave F# Major Arpeggios and Inversions

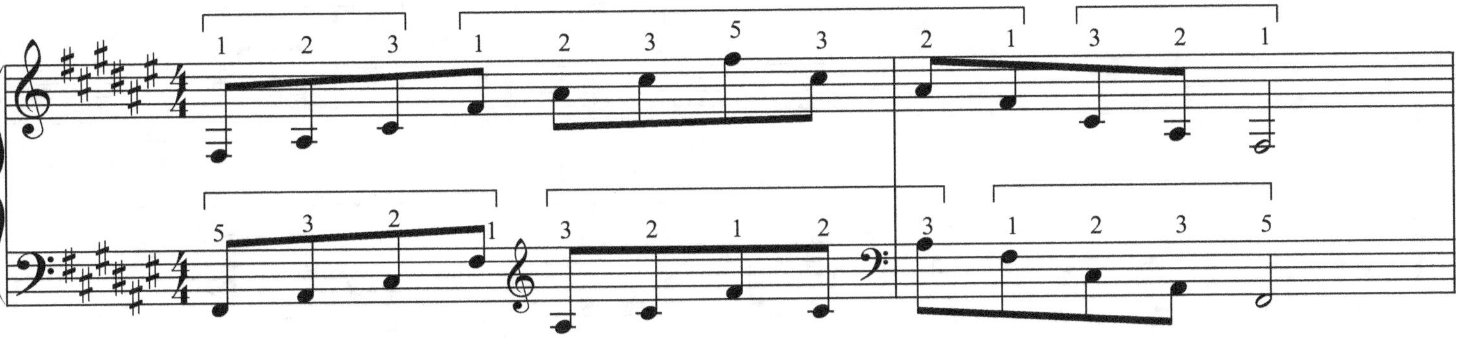

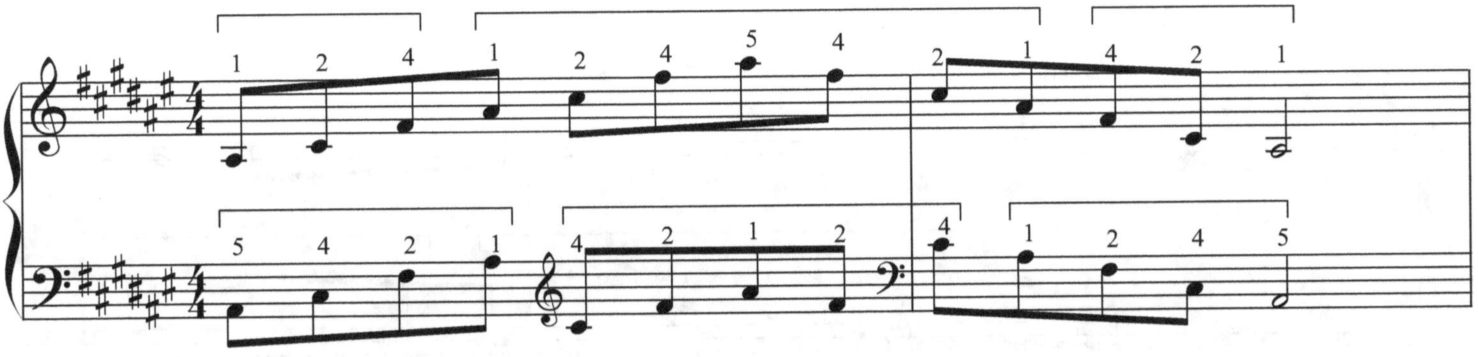

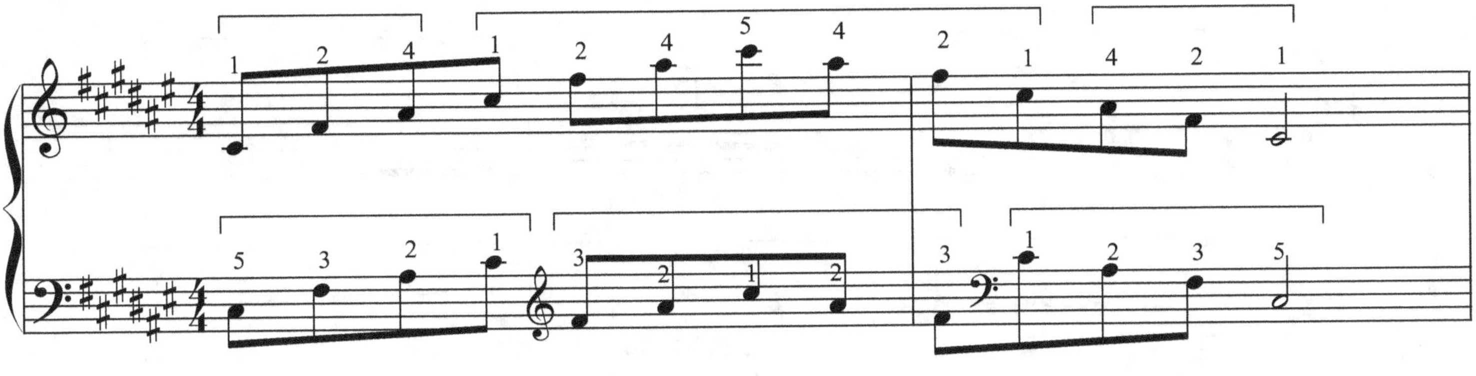

C♯ Major
Enharmonically the same as D♭ - refer to page 59

Two Octave Scale

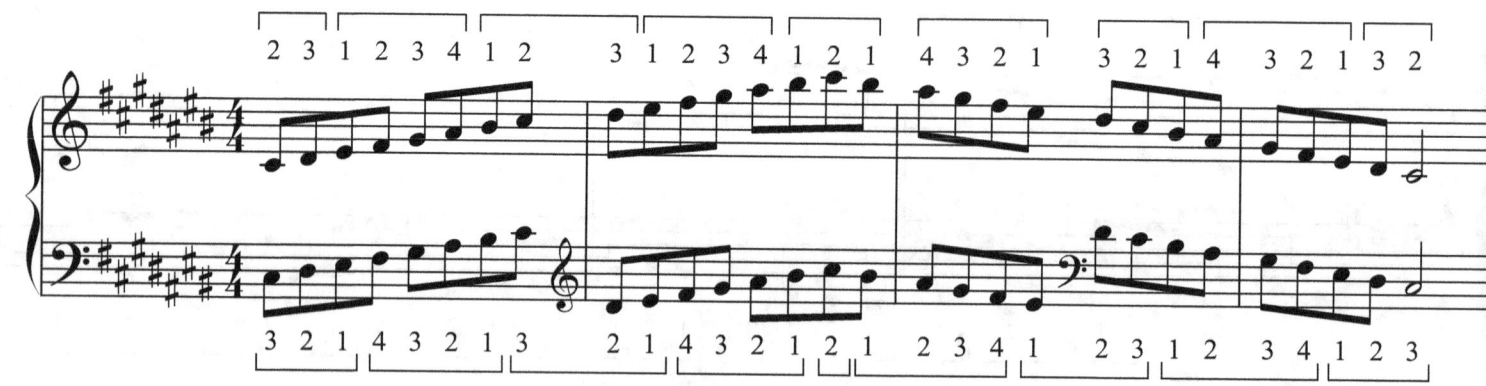

Two Octave C♯ Major Arpeggios and Inversions

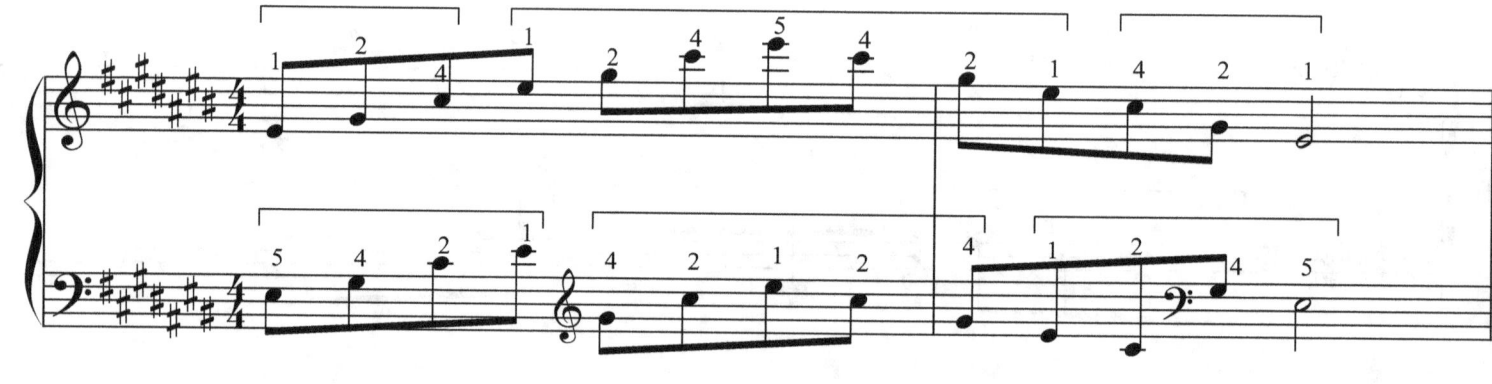

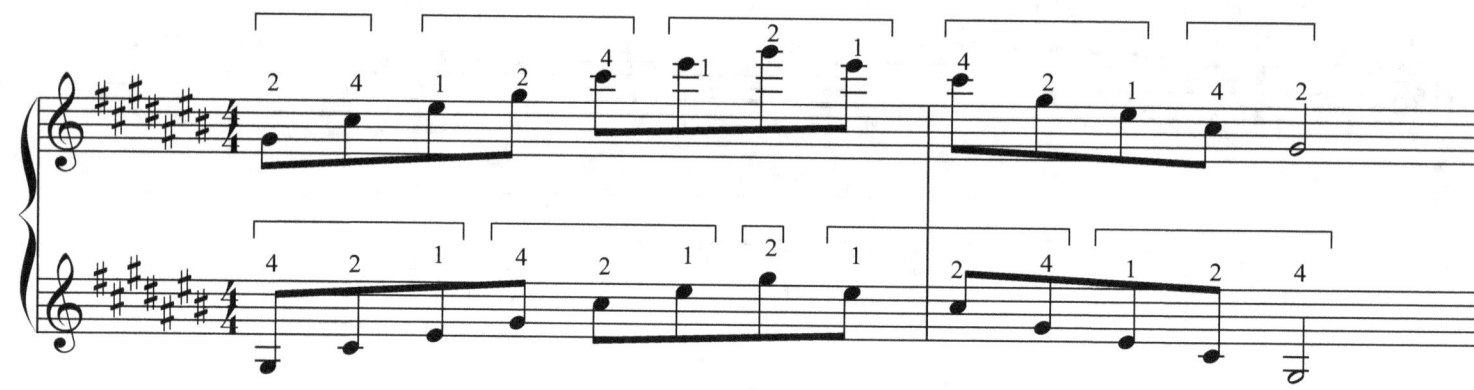

C♭ Major
Enharmonically the same as B - refer to page 39

Two Octave Scale

Two Octave C♭ Major Arpeggios and Inversions

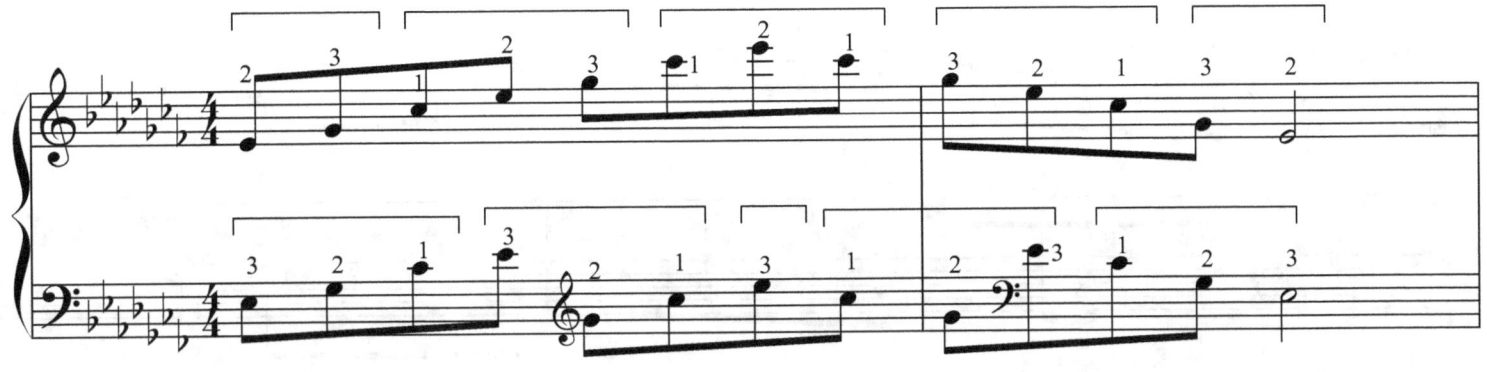

D# Minor

Enharmonically the same as E♭ Minor- refer to page 115

Two Octave Scale

Two Octave D# Minor Arpeggios and Inversions

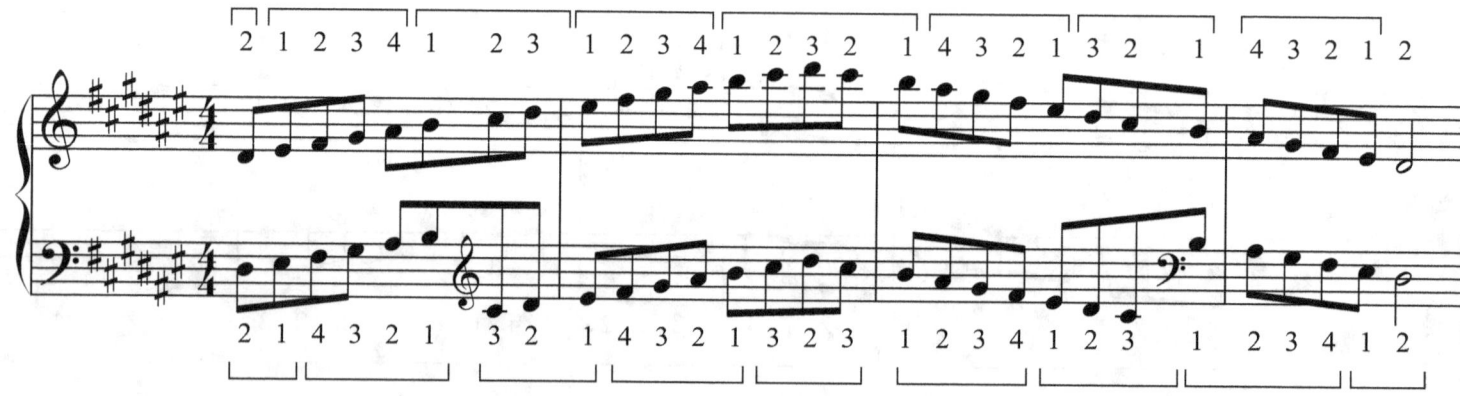

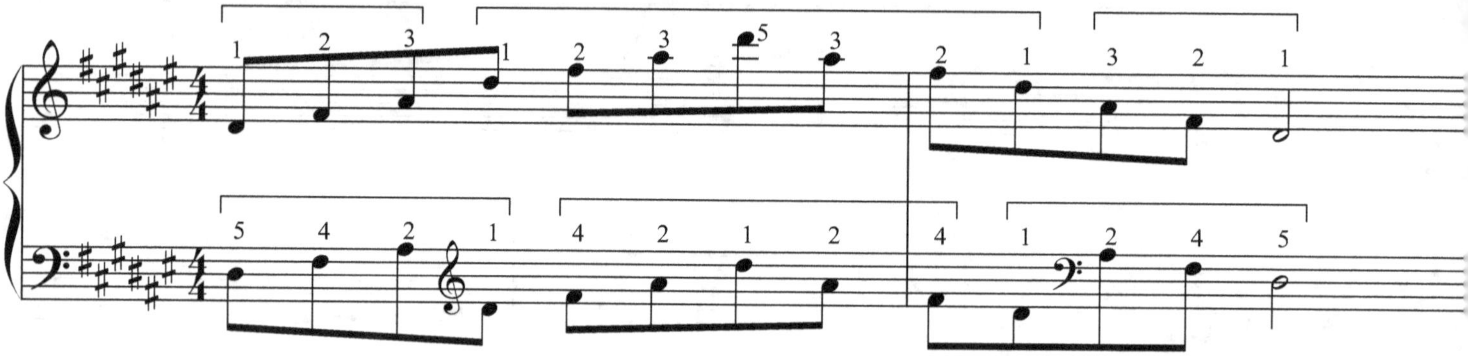

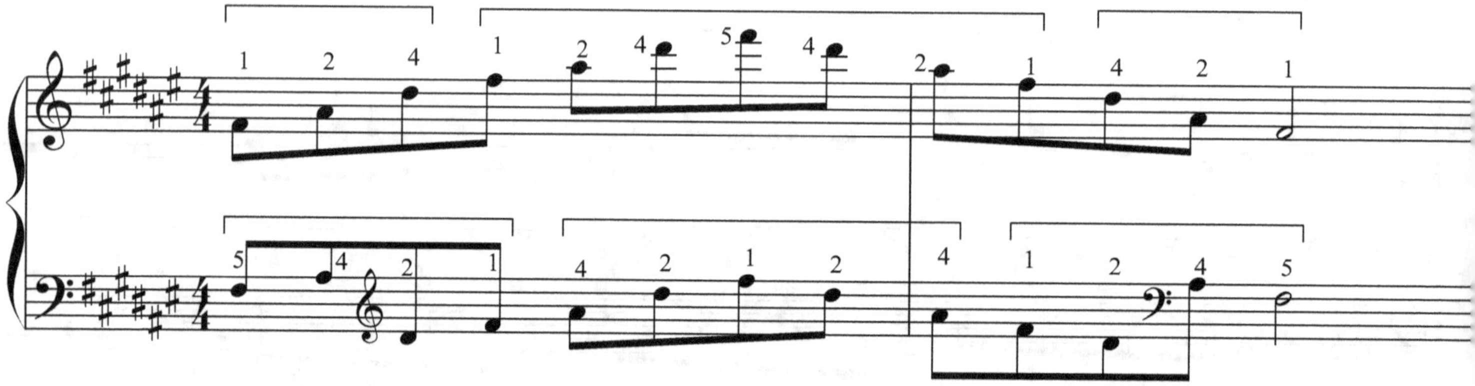

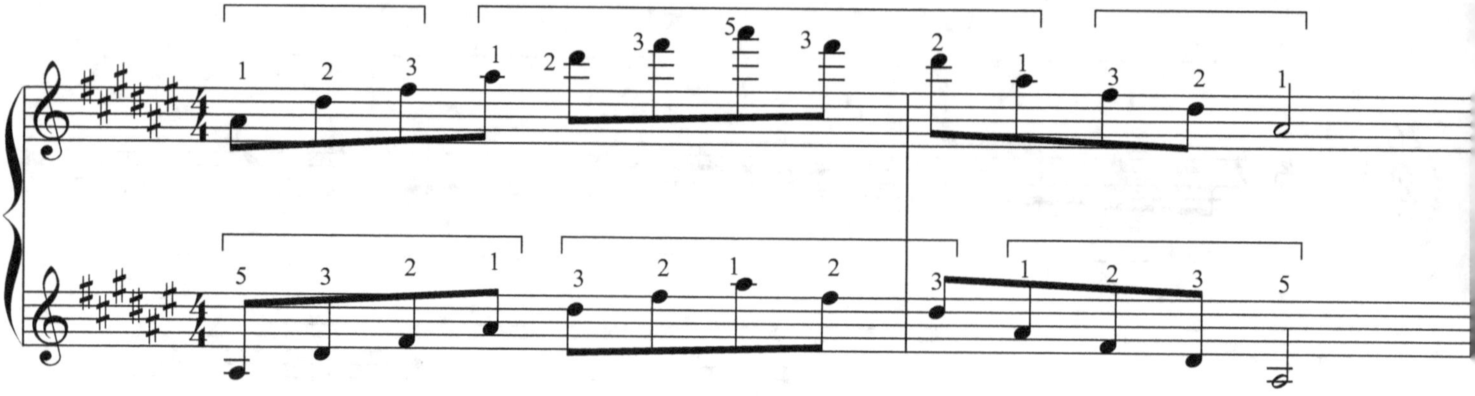

A# Minor

Enharmonically the same as B♭ Minor - refer to page 111

Two Octave Scale

Two Octave A# Minor Arpeggios and Inversions

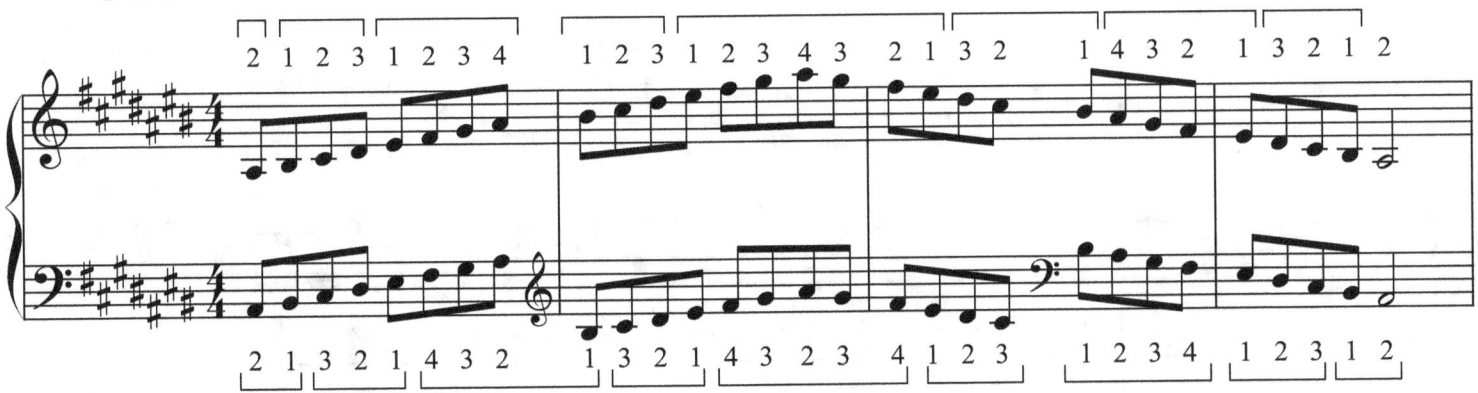

A♭ Minor
Enharmonically the same as G♯ Minor - refer to page 91

Two Octave Scale

Two Octave A♭ Minor Arpeggios and Inversions

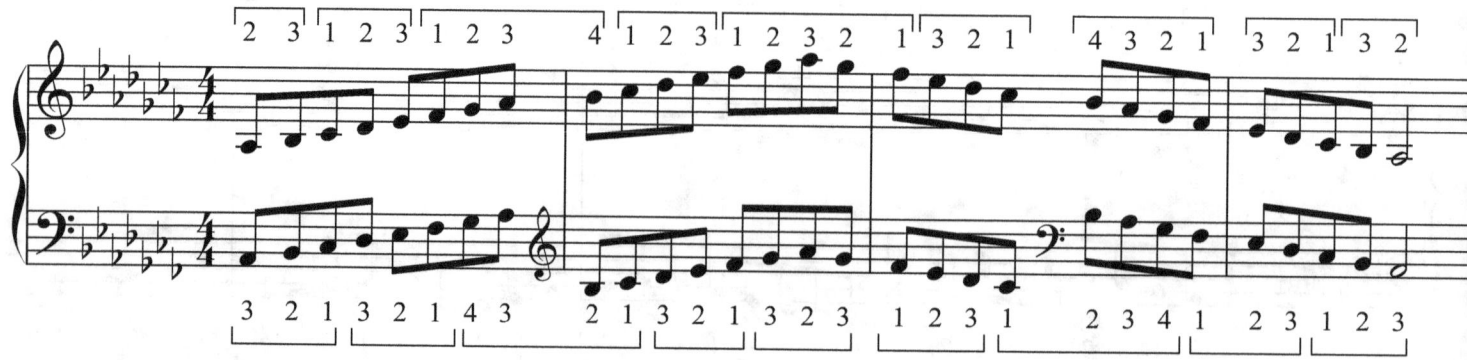